WHO KNEW?

WHO KNEW?

*Responsibility without
Awareness*

GEORGE SHER

OXFORD
UNIVERSITY PRESS

2009

OXFORD

UNIVERSITY PRESS

Oxford University Press, Inc., publishes works that further
Oxford University's objective of excellence
in research, scholarship, and education.

Oxford   New York
Auckland   Cape Town   Dar es Salaam   Hong Kong   Karachi
Kuala Lumpur   Madrid   Melbourne   Mexico City   Nairobi
New Delhi   Shanghai   Taipei   Toronto

With offices in
Argentina   Austria   Brazil   Chile   Czech Republic   France   Greece
Guatemala   Hungary   Italy   Japan   Poland   Portugal   Singapore
South Korea   Switzerland   Thailand   Turkey   Ukraine   Vietnam

Published by Oxford University Press, Inc.
198 Madison Avenue, New York, New York 10016

www.oup.com

Oxford is a registered trademark of Oxford University Press.

Library of Congress Cataloging-in-Publication Data
Sher, George.
Who knew? : responsibility without awareness / George Sher.
p.   cm.
Includes bibliographical references and index.
ISBN 978-0-19-538919-7; 978-0-19-538920-3 (pbk.)
1. Responsibility. 2. Awareness. I. Title.
BJ1451.S52 2009
170'.42—dc22   2008051695

2 4 6 8 9 7 5 3 1
Printed in the United States of America
on acid-free paper

ACKNOWLEDGMENTS

While I was writing this book, I discussed its topics with numerous friends, colleagues, classes, and audiences, and I am pleased to acknowledge their many contributions to the development of my ideas. Those to whom I am indebted include Nomy Arpaly, Baruch Brody, Mark Heller, Neil Levy, Michael McKenna, Donald Morrison, Nicoletta Orlandi, Bernard Rollin, Edward Sherline, Steven Sverdlik, Rachel Zuckert, and the excellent graduate and undergraduate students who were enrolled in my Spring 2008 seminar in moral psychology. I owe a debt of a different order to my wife Emily Fox Gordon, who in addition to being a constant source of encouragement is the best writer I know. Our conversations about writing, hers and mine alike, are a great source of joy to me, and I have benefitted immeasurably from them.

Portions of this book have appeared in an earlier form elsewhere. Parts of chapters 2 and 6 were published in "Out of Control," *Ethics* 116 (January 2006), 285–301. Copyright @ 2006 by the University of Chicago. All rights reserved. Much of chapter 4 was published as "Kantian Fairness" in *Philosophical Issues* 15 (2005), 179–92. @ 2005 Blackwell Publishing. I thank the publishers of those journal for permission to use this material here.

CONTENTS

1. The Searchlight View   3
2. Responsibility without Awareness   23
3. Responsibility and Practical Reason   41
4. Kantian Fairness   55
5. Knew—Or Should Have Known?   71
6. A New Beginning   85
7. Setting the Norms of Recognition   97
8. The Responsible Self   117
9. Out of Control   137

Index   155

WHO KNEW?

ONE

THE SEARCHLIGHT VIEW

I

In the Nicomachean Ethics, Aristotle observed that agents are responsible only for what they do voluntarily—that "[a]cts that are voluntary receive praise and blame, whereas those that are involuntary receive pardon and sometimes pity too."[1] Aristotle also observed that "[a]ctions are regarded as involuntary when they are performed under compulsion or through ignorance."[2] Following Aristotle, most subsequent philosophers have agreed that responsibility has two distinct necessary conditions: one pertaining to the will, the other to knowledge.[3] Although

---

1. Aristotle, *The Ethics of Aristotle: The Nicomachean Ethics*, trans. J. A. K. Thomson (Harmondsworth, England: Penguin, 1955), 111.

2. Aristotle, *The Nicomachean Ethics*, 111.

3. Thus, for example, in the introduction to their influential anthology on the topic, John Martin Fischer and Mark Ravizza have written that "[t]he first condition, which may be termed a 'cognitive condition,' corresponds to the excuse of ignorance. It captures the intuition that an agent is responsible only if she both knows (or can reasonably be expected to know) the particular facts surrounding her action, and also acts with the proper sorts of beliefs and intentions. The second condition, which may be termed a 'freedom-relative condition,' corresponds to the excuse of force. It captures the sense that an agent is responsible only if his action is unforced, that is, only if he acts freely" (John Martin Fischer and Mark Ravizza, eds., *Perspectives on Moral Responsibility* [Ithaca: Cornell University Press, 1993], 8).

these conditions seem equally important, they have not received equal amounts of attention. Because philosophers are preoccupied by determinism, and because determinism threatens freedom more directly than it threatens knowledge, most of what philosophers have said about responsibility has focused on its freedom-related condition. In recent years, they have lavished attention on the question of whether responsibility requires a form of freedom that involves genuine alternative possibilities, and if not what else might distinguish free from unfree acts. By contrast, they have had far less to say about what responsibility requires in the way of knowledge.

In the current book, I propose to reverse this ordering. My central thesis will be that because philosophers have not taken the knowledge requirement seriously, a certain familiar way of understanding it has not received the scrutiny it deserves. To show why we must move beyond this largely unexamined interpretation, I will first reconstruct, and then deconstruct, the sources of its appeal. Then, building on this critical discussion, I will take up the harder task of specifying a viable alternative.

According to the interpretation that I have in mind, an agent's responsibility extends only as far as his awareness of what he is doing. He is responsible only for those acts he consciously chooses to perform, only for those omissions he consciously chooses to allow, and only for those outcomes he consciously chooses to bring about. Because each act has many different properties—here I presuppose a coarse-grained approach to act-individuation[4]—there is an obvious question about which aspects of a given act, omission, or outcome an agent must be aware of in order to be responsible for it. However, to this obvious question, there is an equally obvious answer: namely, that what the agent is responsible for is not his act or omission *simpliciter*, but only those aspects of it and its outcomes of which he *is* aware. Because the

---

4. This approach is taken by G. E. M. Anscombe in *Intention* (Ithaca, NY: Cornell University Press, 1958) and by Donald Davidson in "Actions, Reasons, and Causes," *The Journal of Philosophy* 60 (1963), 685–700, and "The Logical Form of Action Sentences," in Nicholas Rescher, ed., *The Logic of Decision and Action* (Pittsburgh: University of Pittsburgh Press, 1967). For an influential version of the contrasting fine-grained approach, see Alvin H. Goldman, *A Theory of Human Action* (Englewood Cliffs, NJ: Prentice-Hall, 1970).

aspects of a person's acts, omissions, and outcomes that raise questions about his responsibility are precisely those that are morally or prudentially significant, this answer implies that it rarely matters whether an agent is aware that his act involves the contraction of certain muscles or will disturb a fly, but that it often does matter whether he is aware that that act is a lie, that it will hurt someone's feelings, or that it will endanger his own career prospects. The answer also implies that it often matters whether the agent is aware of the range of alternative actions he might perform, of the different outcomes that each action might have, and of the rough likelihoods that the different possible outcomes will eventuate.

Given the many limitations on what we can know, it is impossible for any agent to be aware of every morally and prudentially relevant fact about every act that he might perform. Thus, if being fully responsible requires being aware of all such facts, then no agent is ever fully responsible for what he does. Still, because agents vary widely in the sorts of things of which they are aware, there remains ample room for the view that how much responsibility any given agent has for what he has done is a direct function of the range of relevant facts of which he was aware. This is the view that I want to discuss.

If we accept this view, then we will regard the possibility that an agent might choose among a set of options all of whose morally and prudentially relevant features are fully apparent to him as a kind of limiting case. If, unrealistically, an agent were to make a free choice under these conditions, then the clarity of his vision would guarantee that he was fully responsible both for his act itself and for any good or bad consequences that might flow from it. By contrast, in the more realistic case in which the searchlight of an agent's consciousness does not reach as far as some possible outcome of some available act, the fact that the agent cannot consciously choose either to produce or not to produce that outcome will imply that he cannot be responsible for doing either. Analogously, if the beam of the searchlight is too narrow to illuminate the possibility of performing a certain act, then the fact that the agent cannot consciously choose either to perform or to refrain from performing that act will imply that he cannot be responsible for doing either. Analogously again, if the searchlight's beam is too dim to illuminate some feature that a given act would have, then the fact that the agent cannot consciously choose either to perform or to refrain from performing an act with that feature will similarly excuse him from responsibility for doing either.[5]

Because this view is organized around the metaphor of consciousness as a kind of searchlight, I will from now on refer to it as *the searchlight view*. I will also refer to the corresponding form of control as *searchlight control*. In adopting this terminology, I do not mean to imply that the searchlight view restricts an agent's responsibility to those features of his acts of which he is actively thinking when he performs them. Just as we do not focus our attention on everything that a searchlight illuminates, so too do we not focus it on everything of which we are aware. A driver who is concentrating on not missing his exit may at the same time be aware that a car is approaching on his left, that he is hovering just over the speed limit, that his passenger is telling an anecdote, and of much else. This distinction between active focus and mere awareness is important because the situations in which we make our decisions are generally too complex to enable us to focus simultaneously on each of their morally relevant features. Thus, in its most plausible form, the searchlight view says not that we are responsible only for those features of our acts to which we are actively paying attention, but rather that we are responsible only for those features of which we are at least passively aware.

Even with this refinement, my description of the searchlight view is incomplete in various respects. To mention just one example, the description does not distinguish between a version of the searchlight view that requires only that an agent be aware of whichever features of his choice situation *are in fact* morally and prudentially relevant and a version that also requires that the agent be aware *that* those features are relevant. This distinction is important because the alternative we select will determine exactly how much an agent must be aware of before the searchlight view will count him as responsible for a particular act, omission, or outcome. However, because such refinements will tell us

---

5. Compare J. L. Austin: "Although we have this notion of my idea of what I'm doing—and indeed we have as a general rule such an idea, as it were a miner's lamp on our forehead which illuminates always just so far ahead as we go along—it is not to be supposed that there are any precise rules about the extent and degree of illumination it sheds" (J. L. Austin, "Three Ways of Spilling Ink," *The Philosophical Review* 75 (1966), 438.

only which version of the searchlight view is most plausible, the need to provide them seems less pressing than the need to ascertain whether that view is defensible in principle. If it is, we can always return to fill in the details later.

II

If agents are responsible only for acts they have knowingly and willingly chosen to perform, only for omissions in which they have knowingly and willingly acquiesced, and only for outcomes they have knowingly and willingly chosen to produce, then no one is responsible for any act, omission, or outcome whose moral or prudential defects can be traced to his lack of imagination, his lapses of attention, his poor judgment, or his lack of insight. This means that an agent cannot be responsible for shooting someone if it never occurs to him that his gun may be loaded. It also means that an agent cannot be responsible if, as in the memorable scene in *Pulp Fiction*, his gun discharges when he is casually pointing it at someone in a moving car. However, in fact, we regularly hold people responsible for just such acts. Thus, isn't my claim that many if not most of us accept the searchlight view demonstrably false?

The answer, I think, is that it is not; for what I am claiming is not that we consistently *act as if* the searchlight view were true, but only that the searchlight view informs—and, as I think, distorts—the standard theoretical reconstruction of one widely accepted necessary condition for responsibility. It is, I suggest, the default position to which we gravitate when we are not thinking hard about the knowledge requirement. If, as I hope, my description has elicited a shock of recognition, then no further defense of this suggestion may be required. However, because some readers are bound to remain skeptical, I will offer three pieces of indirect evidence for the view's wide appeal.

One way to appreciate the popularity of the searchlight view is simply to notice how often philosophers assume or presuppose it. Consider, in this regard, the following three quotations:

> [T]he proper immediate objects of moral approval or disapproval would seem to be always the results of a man's volitions insofar as

they were intended—i.e., represented in thought as certain or prob-
able consequences of his volitions...[6]

The careless smoker who has through negligence caused the explosion of a powder keg has not *acted*. On the other hand the worker who
is charged with dynamiting a quarry and who obeys the given orders
has acted when he has produced the expected explosion; he knew
what he was doing or, if you prefer, he intentionally realized a
conscious project.[7]

What an agent wills is a function of her grasp of a situation. If it is
willings that are the object of moral assessment, judgments of right
and wrong will then reflect the perspective of the agent, and so be
relative to what she sees or considers relevant in the circumstances in
which she acts.[8]

Although Henry Sidgwick, Jean-Paul Sartre, and Barbara Herman hold
very different philosophical views—they are, respectively, a utilitarian,
an existentialist, and a Kantian—each here implies that an agent is
responsible only for what he is aware of doing.

That same implication, moreover, can also be extracted from a
certain familiar reaction to the phenomena of negligence and culpable
ignorance. To make sense of the fact that agents can be blameworthy,
and hence responsible, for acts that they do not recognize as wrong,
many people assume that each such agent must previously have knowingly assumed the *risk* of doing something wrong. For example, in the
case of the agent who does not realize that his gun is loaded, they
assume that he must at some point have made a conscious decision
not to bother to check. As Michael J. Zimmerman has put the point,
"all culpability can be traced to culpability that involves lack of ignorance, that is, that involves a belief on the agent's part that he or she is
doing something morally wrong."[9] I believe, and will argue at length

6. Henry Sidgwick, *The Methods of Ethics*, 7th edition (Indianapolis: Hackett, 1981), 60.

7. Jean-Paul Sartre, *Being and Nothingness*, H. E. Barnes, trans. (New York: Philosophical Library, 1956), 433.

8. Barbara Herman, *The Practice of Moral Judgment* (Cambridge, MA: Harvard University Press, 1993), 95.

9. Michael J. Zimmerman, "Moral Responsibility and Ignorance," *Ethics* 107 (April
1997), 418.

below, that this claim is badly mistaken, but what matters for present purposes is not its truth but only its popularity. Whenever anyone explains how an agent can be blameworthy for an unwitting wrong act by postulating an earlier wrong act that he *was* aware of performing, he attests to the pull of the idea that an agent's control, and so too his responsibility, extends no further than his conscious choices.

My last piece of indirect evidence for the searchlight view's popularity is the common belief that an agent is responsible only for those aspects of his behavior that are voluntary in the sense of being expressions of his *will*. The reason this belief is relevant is that will appears to be essentially a conscious phenomenon. Although it is clearly coherent to speak of unconscious beliefs, desires, and choices, it is not clearly coherent—indeed, I think it is clearly *not* coherent—to speak of an unconscious exercise of will. Whatever willing comes to, it appears to be something we must be aware of doing whenever we do it. For this reason, it is hard to see how the beliefs upon which we base our acts of will can be anything but conscious either. And, because of this, the common tendency to understand voluntariness in terms of will is yet a third piece of evidence for the popularity of the searchlight view.

III

Despite its pervasiveness, I think we must reject the searchlight view. To set the stage both for my critical discussion and for the development of a more adequate alternative, I will begin with a diagnosis of what I take to be the fundamental problem.

Put most briefly, the basic difficulty with the searchlight view is that it conflates two different and incompatible perspectives on action. The two perspectives that I have in mind are, first, the engaged perspective that we occupy when we ourselves act, and, second, the detached perspective that we occupy when we consider people's acts—our own or those of others—"from the outside." My reason for thinking that the searchlight view conflates these perspectives is that it draws on a conception of the agent that derives its plausibility from the first perspective while purporting to specify a necessary condition for the applicability of a concept—responsibility—whose natural home is the second.

Let me elaborate these claims, beginning with the claim that the searchlight view draws on a conception of the agent that derives its plausibility from the perspective of agency. My reason for saying this is that when we engage with the world as agents—when we see ourselves as having to decide what to do, weigh the reasons for and against the acts we might perform, make our decisions on the basis of these reasons, and so on—the process as we encounter it is at every stage fully conscious. We can only deliberate about the possibilities as we see them, can only weigh the significance of the facts as we know them, and can only base our decisions on our reasons as we understand them. Because deliberation is conscious through and through, anyone who engages in it—that is, each of us, all the time—must encounter himself simply as a (volitionally effective) center of consciousness. Even if we are aware that we hold many beliefs of which we are not aware, we must view those beliefs as inaccessible to us and hence as irrelevant to whatever practical question we are trying to answer. Small wonder, then, that from the deliberative perspective, we see our options, and thus also ourselves insofar as we are the ones who must choose among those options, as bounded by our own consciousness.

But whereas the deliberative perspective is naturally associated with a maximally narrow view of ourselves, the perspective from which questions of responsibility arise is equally naturally associated with a much wider view. When we ask whether someone is responsible for what he did, we presuppose that the act in question has already been performed, and hence that its performance is not an option for us. Even when we ourselves are the ones who have acted, our current perspective, which is both retrospective and disengaged, is very different from the perspective that we occupied when the issue was in doubt. From where we now stand, the practical question is not whether we should perform the act, but at most how we should react to its performance. To answer the latter question, we must consider all potentially relevant facts, including any that were inaccessible to the agent when he made his decision. Hence, from this perspective, there is no *a priori* reason to exclude those states of the agent that were not illuminated by the searchlight of his consciousness.

The perspective of the agent and that of the person who encounters his actions from the outside are incompatible in the sense that no one can simultaneously occupy them both. However, the two perspectives are not incompatible in the stronger sense that occupying one prevents us from taking account of how things appear from the other. Because the two perspectives remain compatible in the latter sense, the fact that we can only assess an agent's responsibility from an external and disengaged perspective does not show that our assessment cannot depend entirely on how things appeared to him from his internal and engaged perspective. Even if our external perspective does not itself compel us to ignore all cognitive states to which the agent lacked access, there may be further considerations, specific to the theory of responsibility, that compel us to do just this.

Are there any such considerations? This, in my opinion, is the deepest question about the searchlight view, and the one on which its tenability depends. The considerations that either suggest themselves as relevant or have actually been put forth in this connection are quite diverse. They include the alleged practical nature of the concept of responsibility, the unfairness of blaming or punishing people for what they cannot help, the connection between imaginatively identifying with an agent and understanding what he has done, and the unreasonableness of any demand with which the agent to whom it is directed is unable to comply. However, although there is obviously much to say about each consideration, I believe, and will argue below, that none of them implies that holding an agent responsible requires regarding what he did exclusively from his own perspective. That is why I have described the searchlight view as conflating, as opposed to being rationally dictated by the need to integrate, the agent's perspective and our own.

By drawing attention to this conflation, I hope not only to undermine the searchlight view's appeal, but also to lay the groundwork for a more adequate interpretation of the knowledge requirement. Put most simply, the moral I wish to draw is that instead of taking an agent's responsibility to be a simple function of what he consciously believed when he acted, we must take it to be a more complex function of his conscious beliefs on the one hand and certain objective facts about him and his situation on the other. Although the state of his consciousness when he acted is bound to remain significant, the significance of the different things of which he was aware is bound to depend on facts of which in their turn he was *not* aware.

The harder task, of course, is to make these claims precise. What needs to be explained is exactly what mixture of subjective and objective elements is involved and exactly why a mixture of that sort should add up to the kind of cognitive state that is necessary for responsibility. To bring out the difficulty of these questions, let us return briefly to our gun example. As we saw, any interpretation of the knowledge requirement that seeks to do justice to our intuitions about responsibility must imply that an agent to whom it simply does not occur that his gun may be loaded may nevertheless know enough about his situation to be responsible when he shoots someone. However, at the same time, such an interpretation must also imply that an agent who shoots someone is *not* responsible for doing so if, for example, he is an actor whom the prop manager has mistakenly handed a loaded gun, or if he has been deceived into thinking the bullets are blanks. But what, exactly, is the difference between an agent who is merely oblivious to the danger and one who has been misled or deceived? What cognitive relation between the agent and the fact that his gun is loaded is present in the case of the oblivious shooter but absent in the cases of the actor and the victim of deception? What is it about the facts that account for these agents' lack of awareness that sustains an attribution of responsibility in the first case but fails to do so in the second or third? These are the questions around which the second half of the book will be organized. By taking them seriously, I will attempt to work my way to a constructive alternative to the searchlight view.

IV

So far, I have treated responsibility as a unified concept. However, given the many contexts in which we speak of people (and things) as responsible, we cannot take the concept's unity for granted. For this reason, we also cannot assume that the necessary conditions for responsibility are always the same. Thus, before I proceed to a sketch of my argument, I must say something about its intended scope.

Even if we set aside all merely causal attributions of responsibility—that is, even if we disregard all assertions such as "mental fatigue was responsible for the crash"—the attributions that remain will straddle two cross-cutting distinctions. On the one hand, we view agents as responsible sometimes for the morally, sometimes for the prudentially relevant features of their actions; on the other, we view them as responsible sometimes for acts that meet or exceed, sometimes for acts that fall decisively below, the relevant moral or prudential standards. Combined, the two distinctions yield four different contexts in which we attribute responsibility. We do so whenever we (1) blame an agent for acting wrongly; (2) praise an agent for exceeding his duty or doing the right thing under difficult circumstances; (3) criticize an agent for acting foolishly or self-destructively; or (4) give an agent credit for his success in achieving some aim.

Of the four contexts just cited, it is the first, which involves wrongdoing, that has received the most attention. Questions about excuses, to which the knowledge requirement is proffered as a partial answer, arise mainly in this context. However, although the knowledge requirement is mentioned most often in connection with wrongdoing, it clearly applies in the other three contexts too. Just as we withdraw our blame when we learn that an agent could not have known that he was doing something hurtful or saying something false, so too do we withdraw our commendation when we discover that, for example, the soldier who advanced fearlessly toward the enemy had no way of knowing that he was in danger. So too, again, do we withdraw our charge of poor planning when we learn that our unprepared student was given a wrong date for his exam; and so too, finally, do we withdraw our admiration when we learn that our prosperous friend bases his stock purchases simply on the attractiveness of the companies' names.

In all four cases, the discovery that the agent was ignorant of a certain aspect of his situation compels us to acknowledge that he is not responsible for the corresponding feature of what he did. In all four cases, too, the discovery that the agent was not acting freely would have a similar effect. Because both necessary conditions apply across the board, it is natural to assume that the operative concept of responsibility is the same in each context, and hence that the case for accepting or rejecting the searchlight view is the same as well. I think, in fact, that these assumptions are correct, but I also think that we cannot accept them without facing up to two complications, one that concerns the distinction between moral and prudential responsibility and one that arises when we consider the difference between positive and negative cases.

The first of these complications is raised by an analysis that has been put forth by Thomas Scanlon. According to Scanlon, there is an important difference between moral responsibility and responsibility for one's good or bad fortunes (he refers to these, respectively, as responsibility as attributability and substantive responsibility). Though superficially similar, the two forms of responsibility reflect quite different concerns and have quite different normative roots. Put most simply, the difference is that

> When we ask whether a person is responsible in the first of these senses for a given action, what we are asking is whether that person is properly subject to praise or blame for having acted in that way. To say that someone is responsible in the second sense for a certain outcome is . . . to say that that person cannot complain of the burdens or obligations that result. . . . Judgments of responsibility in the second sense . . . are substantive conclusions about what we owe to each other.[10]

Scanlon's distinction between responsibility as attributability and substantive responsibility corresponds closely to my own distinction between moral and prudential responsibility. Thus, if Scanlon is correct in saying that his two forms of responsibility have different normative roots, then even if moral and prudential responsibility both require that the relevant agents know what they are doing, the senses in which they require this may well be different. In this way, Scanlon's proposal is a potential threat to my project of articulating a single broadly applicable alternative to the searchlight view.

To assess the magnitude of the threat, let us consider an example that Scanlon introduces to illustrate his notion of substantive responsibility. Scanlon asks us to imagine a case in which a city is seeking to dispose of some toxic waste. Although the public has been warned to avoid the waste disposal site, and although the city's warning is sufficient in the sense that no more is required by a principle that no one could reasonably reject, there remain some who do not stay away and as a result suffer lung damage. Intuitively, it seems that because the city has given warning which by hypothesis was ample, it is not responsible for this damage. The crucial question, however, is exactly *why* the city is not responsible.

One possible answer, which Scanlon dubs "the forfeiture view," is that the victims have forfeited their right to complain by choosing to

---

10. Thomas Scanlon, *What We Owe to Each Other* (Cambridge, MA: Harvard University Press, 1998), 290.

take the risk. According to the forfeiture view, the reason the city is *not* responsible is that the injured citizens *are* responsible because of what they did. If this view is correct, then a person's responsibility for his bad fortune, no less than his moral responsibility, will be a function of his actions, and so my conjecture that both forms of responsibility share a single epistemic condition will indeed be plausible. However, for a number of reasons, Scanlon thinks we should reject the forfeiture view. For one thing, although certain victims did choose to take the risk— some did so impulsively or carelessly while others acted rationally in light of their circumstances—there are also some who just never got the word. Because these uninformed victims have done nothing to forfeit their right to complain, the city's lack of responsibility for their injuries cannot be grounded in any such forfeiture. In addition, even in the case of those who did choose to take the risk, Scanlon argues that the best explanation of why the city is not responsible is not that the injured parties made this choice, but is simply that it did everything that was required by a principle that no one can reasonably reject.

Let us grant that Scanlon is right about this. Let us grant, in other words, that the reason the city is not responsible for compensating the victims has nothing to do with what *they* did and everything to do with what *it* did.[11] Even so, there is surely another form of responsibility that *does* depend on what the victims did. This is evident from the fact that we can plausibly say of both the rational and the careless victims that they themselves are responsible for incurring the harm while we clearly cannot say this about the victims who simply never got the word. Only the rational and the careless victims, but not the ones who never received the crucial information, are responsible for making the choices that *caused* the damage. When I speak of moral and nonmoral

---

11. For discussion of an interestingly different view, see Susan Hurley, *Justice, Luck, and Knowledge* (Cambridge, MA: Harvard University Press, 2003). Hurley's topic is the popular view that "distributive justice should respect differences between people's positions for which they are responsible but should neutralize differences that are a matter of luck" (1), and she explicitly stipulates that "'responsibility' is intended in the full-blooded sense that licenses praise, blame, and reactive attitudes and that implies accountability in principle" (4). Thus, according to the view that Hurley is discussing, the reason the city is not responsible for the damage to the victims may indeed be located in their actions rather than its own.

responsibility as different species of a single genus, it is only this form of nonmoral responsibility that I have in mind.[12] Because moral responsibility and this form of nonmoral responsibility do seem continuous, they are indeed likely to share a common set of necessary conditions. Thus, despite Scanlon's illuminating discussion, we may continue to assume that any cogent criticism of the searchlight view, and any cogent alternative to it, will apply in the nonmoral as well as the moral context.

Is it also reasonable to assume that any adequate account will apply in both the positive and the negative contexts? This question is harder to answer than the first because our intuitions about the positive and negative contexts differ in significant ways. For example, although we intuitively believe that an agent who does not realize that his gun is loaded may nevertheless deserve blame for shooting someone with it, we do *not* believe that such an agent is deserving of praise if his weapon discharges without harming anyone and thereby scares off a burglar. In light of this and other asymmetries, the claim that the epistemic requirement is the same in both contexts cannot be taken for granted, but must be argued for. However, because the negative context is by far the more important, I will defer my treatment of this issue until much later in the book. In the chapters that follow, I will concentrate exclusively on trying to understand the epistemic condition for responsibility as it pertains to agents who act wrongly or imprudently. Then, once the more important cases have been accounted for, I will go on to show how what has been said also applies, albeit with suitable modifications, to agents whose acts are morally or nonmorally praiseworthy.

---

12. By distinguishing this form of nonmoral responsibility from what Scanlon calls substantive responsibility, we open up the possibility that the allocative principles that determine people's substantive responsibility may themselves be grounded in premises about the other form of nonmoral responsibility. It may be the case, that is, that everyone has reason to opt for a set of allocative principles that place a higher priority on the mitigation of self-inflicted harms for which agents are *not* responsible than on the mitigation of self-inflicted harms for which agents *are* responsible. I think, in fact, that this priority ordering is very plausible, but because my topic is responsibility and not justice, I will not pursue the suggestion further.

V

With these matters clarified, I can turn to the promised outline of the book's argument. Its basic structure is simple enough: chapters 2–4 will press various criticisms of the searchlight view, chapter 5 will explore an inadequate alternative to that view, and chapters 6–9 will motivate and develop what I take to be a more adequate alternative.

The most straightforward way to show that all is not well with the searchlight view is to establish that it conflicts with many of our ground-level beliefs about who is responsible for what. Although I have already hinted at this, I will make the argument in much more detail in chapter 2. To do so, I will begin by presenting nine examples of agents who are unaware of the morally relevant features of their wrong acts or omissions, yet who still seem morally responsible for those acts or omissions. Of these examples, some involve lapses of attention, some poor judgment, and some a lack of moral insight or imagination. Although not every reader will accept every example—different readers, I suspect, will take issue with different ones—their cumulative thrust will be that taking the searchlight view seriously would mean drastically revising many of our judgments about which agents are morally responsible for what. In addition, by proposing a variant of each case in which the agent harms only himself, I will argue that taking the searchlight view seriously would also require drastic revisions in our judgments about which agents are *non*morally responsible for what. Then, to conclude the chapter, I will provide the reasoning that vindicates my earlier expression of disdain for the view that each culpably ignorant agent has previously made a conscious choice to risk unwittingly acting wrongly.

Just how strongly these counterintuitive implications of the searchlight view tell against it will of course depend on the strength of the countervailing arguments. Thus, the natural next question is how strong a case can be made *for* the searchlight view. There are, I think, two main possible lines of argument, each of which appeals to the already-noted fact that we can only deliberate about those features of the available actions of which we are aware. One way to deploy this fact in defense of the searchlight view is to argue that because responsibility is a practical concept—because it is precisely when we deliberate that we are compelled to regard ourselves as responsible for whatever choices we make—the preconditions for responsibility must also be supplied *by* the deliberative perspective. An alternative but complementary strategy is to argue that holding an agent responsible for a feature of his act of which he was not antecedently aware, and about which he therefore could not deliberate, is wrong because it is *unfair*. These two arguments will be discussed, respectively, in chapters 3 and 4.

Where the first argument is concerned, the central question is why the concept of responsibility to which deliberation commits us must be applicable not only to us when we deliberate, but also to us at other, later times and to other people. Even if the choices that we now think we would be responsible for if we made them can extend no further than the options of which we are now aware, why should the actions for which we view ourselves as responsible in retrospect be similarly restricted by our earlier perspective? And why, a fortiori, should the same restriction apply when we hold other people responsible for what *they* have done? To assess the prospects for answering this question, I will structure chapter 3 around the attempts of the two main proponents of the view that responsibility is a practical concept, Christine Korsgaard and Hilary Bok, to bridge the future–past and self–other gaps. Reduced to their essentials, my conclusions will be that (a) the viability of each philosopher's attempt to bridge each gap depends on the answers to various further questions, but that (b) even if those attempts succeed, they do not preserve the original rationale for supposing that a practical concept of responsibility applies only to features of acts of which agents are aware.

This last conclusion strongly suggests that the searchlight view cannot be grounded exclusively in the requirements of the deliberative perspective. However, it might still be possible to ground the searchlight view in a combination of premises that includes both the requirements of the deliberative perspective and some independently defensible normative principle. There is, moreover, one particular normative principle that seems especially well suited to fill this role. This is the principle that holding people responsible (blaming them, punishing them) for acts, omissions, or outcomes over which they lack control is wrong because it is unfair. For reasons that will become clear, I will refer to this as *The Kantian Principle*. In chapter 4, I will explore its connection to the searchlight view.

Most people would accept some version of the Kantian Principle. However, before a proponent of the searchlight view can appeal to this principle, he will have to defend a certain interpretation of its key notions of fairness and control. More specifically, he will have to show that at least one defensible interpretation of the principle's notion of fairness compels us to interpret its notion of control in terms of conscious awareness. Unfortunately, because the exact content of the Kantian Principle is rarely discussed, we cannot evaluate the prospects for showing this by examining what other philosophers have said. Thus, to move the discussion forward, I will first propose, and then criticize, what seem to me the two most promising reasons for accepting the requisite interpretations.

Of these reasons, the first is that holding someone responsible involves imaginatively entering into that person's own perspective—a perspective from which any demand of which he is unaware is indeed bound to seem unfair. The second is that holding someone responsible involves the retrospective endorsement of a demand that could only have been effective if it was antecedently intelligible *from* the agent's perspective. Because both reasons make ineliminable reference to the deliberating agent's perspective, each nicely captures the thought that the demands of that perspective are bound to play some central role in any adequate justification of the searchlight view. Nevertheless, despite their initial promise, I will argue that both reasons collapse under pressure. This will leave us with no obvious way of defending the only version of the Kantian Principle upon which an argument for the searchlight view can rest. Thus, pending some further and better defense of the searchlight view—and none, in my opinion, is even on the horizon—my conclusion will be that that view's highly counterintuitive consequences tell decisively against it.

If this conclusion is correct, then we will have to interpret the epistemic condition for responsibility in some other way. But what form, exactly, might an alternative interpretation take? To work my way to an answer, I will begin by considering the familiar proposal that when someone acts wrongly or foolishly, the question on which his responsibility depends is not whether he *is* aware that his act is wrong or foolish, but rather whether he *should* be (or, alternatively, whether a reasonable person in his position *would* be). Like the searchlight view, this proposal makes essential reference to the agent's epistemic situation; but unlike the searchlight view, it correctly distinguishes between, for example, the shooter who simply does not realize that his gun is loaded and the actor who is handed a loaded gun as a prop. It is, for these reasons, the natural place to begin.

Despite its obvious advantages, I will argue in chapter 5 that this proposal cannot stand on its own. Put most simply, the central problem is that on any reasonable interpretation of the proposal's "should," the truth of the claim that an agent should be aware that he is acting wrongly or foolishly will depend exclusively on some combination of facts about the evidence to which he has access and his failure to respond adequately to that evidence. Conspicuously absent from these truth-makers will be any facts about the agent that might *account for* the inadequacy of his response to the evidence. This last omission is crucial because it leaves us without an explanation of how the agent's cognitive failure—which is, after all, a mere nonoccurrence—can have the positive effect of rendering him responsible for the ensuing act.

To rectify this omission, we need not abandon the claim that agents are responsible only for those wrong or foolish acts of whose relevant features they should have been aware, but we do need to augment that claim with an explanation of when and why an agent's cognitive failure is attributable to *him*. At first glance, we may be tempted to say that such a failure is attributable to the agent when and because it reflects his conscious choice. However, to say that each negligent agent has consciously chosen not to recognize the features that make his act wrong or foolish would be to reintroduce the searchlight view at yet another point. It would also commit us to the pervasive occurrence of an especially paradoxical form of self-deception. Thus, it is precisely at this juncture that we seem forced to go external. To connect an agent to his unwitting wrong or foolish act in a way that is strong enough to sustain the judgment that he is responsible for performing it, we will have to trace his failure to recognize the act's wrongness or foolishness to some fact about him that can in principle be identified from a perspective independent of his own. Beginning in chapter 6, I will attempt to do just that.

Put most simply, my proposal will be that when an agent performs an act of whose wrongness or foolishness he should be but is not aware, what connects him to this cognitive failure is that the failure is itself explicable in terms of the interactions among the innumerable desires, beliefs, attitudes, and dispositions, many of them unconscious, that together make him the individual he is. Unlike a nonculpably ignorant agent, who simply lacks any information that would support the conclusion that he is acting wrongly, the culpably ignorant agent does have the necessary information, but is prevented by some aspect of his character or belief-system from putting the pieces together. Underlying this proposal is the idea that the agents to whom we attribute responsibility are not just conscious centers of will, but rather are complex beings whose identity depends on—indeed, who are partly constituted by—a vast array of attitudes and traits to which they themselves lack access.[13] Although this view of the self is of course familiar, its bearing on the theory of responsibility has not been sufficiently appreciated. By adopting a suitably broad conception of the responsible agent, we may also hope to broaden our understanding of how he is connected to what he unwittingly does.

According to the view that I will propose, an agent is not responsible for an act of whose wrongness or foolishness he is unaware unless (1) his failure to recognize the act as wrong or foolish falls short of satisfying some applicable standard, and (2) his failure to satisfy that standard is in turn accounted for by some combination of his constitutive attitudes and traits. To defend my proposal, I will therefore have to discuss both the standards that determine what someone in a given agent's situation should be aware of and the attitudes and traits by which I take such an agent to be constituted. My discussion of the standards is organized around two crosscutting distinctions: first, between the situations to which they apply and the agents who must act in those situations, and, second, between genuine norms and mere statistical regularities. To play the role that I have assigned them, the relevant standards cannot classify too many of the determinants of an agent's cognitive failure as aspects of his situation, and they must have genuine normative force. The claim that the standards are genuinely normative will be explicated and defended in chapter 7. However, because the question of which causal factors are part of an agent's situation depends on how we understand the boundaries of the self, the task of demarcating the agent from his situation will be left for chapter 8.

---

13. In a number of important respects, including both its downplaying of the first-person perspective and the role that it assigns to the responsible agent's character, the general tenor of my account is Humean rather than Kantian. For Hume himself on responsibility, see David Hume, *A Treatise of Human Nature*, ed. L. A. Selby-Bigge (Oxford: Oxford University Press), book II, part III, sec. II.

In that chapter, I will defend a conception of the responsible self that stands somewhere between the maximalist view that such selves are simply full human beings none of whose physical or psychological features are any more essential than any others, and the minimalist view that when people are considered under the aspect of responsibility, they are constituted only by those features—consciousness and reason-responsiveness are the two main candidates—that are general prerequisites for it. To capture what is best about each approach, I will argue that each responsible self is constituted not only by the conscious states and rational judgments in whose absence questions about his responsibility would not arise, but also by the (presumably very substantial) subset of his other physical and psychological states whose causal interaction *sustains* the crucial states and judgments. Because this view of the responsible self seems independently defensible, and because it dovetails neatly with the only reconstruction of responsibility's epistemic condition that does justice to our full range of judgments about who is responsible for what, the different elements of my proposal will turn out to hang together in a satisfying way.

A number of questions, however, remain unresolved. For one thing, because chapters 6–8 deal only with the conditions under which agents are responsible for unwitting acts that are wrong and foolish, it remains to be seen whether, and if so how, the proposed account can be extended to accommodate the very different conditions under which agents are responsible for unwitting acts that are right and prudent. A second outstanding question concerns the relation between responsibility's epistemic and voluntariness conditions: how, if responsibility does not require awareness, can it require that the features of a person's acts for which he is responsible be expressions of his will? Yet a third question, closely related to this one, is whether an account which implies that agents can be responsible for features of their acts of which they are unaware must abandon the familiar view that responsibility requires control. In the book's ninth and final chapter, I shall propose answers to each of these questions. Although these answers will require some adjustment of some common beliefs, we will have to abandon only certain inessential accretions that can be traced to indefensible theoretical commitments. As compensation, we will gain a clearer view of what responsibility must be—a view that manages to acknowledge its connection to reason and subjectivity without denying that its subjects are located squarely in the natural world.

TWO

RESPONSIBILITY WITHOUT AWARENESS

MY AIM IN THIS CHAPTER IS TO DOCUMENT THE STRIKING CONTRAST between the standard way of understanding responsibility's epistemic condition—the interpretation I have dubbed "the searchlight view"— and our actual ground-level judgments about who is responsible for what. To make this disparity vivid, I will begin by introducing nine cases in which agents seem blameworthy, and hence morally responsible, for acts of whose wrongness they are unaware.[1] After I discuss these cases, which will serve as my touchstone in the chapters to come, I will propose a variant of each case in which the agent acts imprudently rather than wrongly, and will generalize what has been said in a number of directions. Then, with the problem fully before us, I will argue against two attempts to avoid the difficulty by relocating the acts for which the unwitting wrongdoers and foolish agents are responsible to earlier points in their histories.

I

There are many ways in which agents can fail to recognize the morally relevant features of their potential acts. Although the categories are

---

1. Here and elsewhere in the chapter, I will use "acts" in a broad sense that encompasses omissions as well as positive actions.

somewhat fluid, we can usefully distinguish between cases in which an agent acts wrongly because he forgets or loses track of some crucial element of his situation, cases in which he does so because he exercises poor judgment, and cases in which the problem lies in his lack of moral insight or imagination. As a first step toward documenting my claim that the searchlight view systematically fails to capture our intuitions about responsibility, I will argue that we often hold agents responsible in all three contexts.

Here, first, are three cases in which agents seem responsible for wrong acts that they performed because they forgot or otherwise lost track of crucial elements of their situation:

1. *Hot Dog*. Alessandra, a soccer mom, has gone to pick up her children at their elementary school. As usual, Alessandra is accompanied by the family's border collie, Bathsheba, who rides in the back of the van. Although it is very hot, the pick-up has never taken long, so Alessandra leaves Sheba in the van while she goes to gather her children. This time, however, Alessandra is greeted by a tangled tale of misbehavior, ill-considered punishment, and administrative bungling which requires several hours of indignant sorting out. During that time, Sheba languishes, forgotten, in the locked car. When Alessandra and her children finally make it to the parking lot, they find Sheba unconscious from heat prostration.

2. *On the Rocks*. Julian, a ferry pilot, is nearing the end of a forty-minute trip that he has made hundreds of times before. The only challenge in this segment of the trip is to avoid some submerged rocks that jut out irregularly from the mainland. However, just because the trip is so routine, Julian's thoughts have wandered to the previous evening's pleasant romantic encounter. Too late, he realizes that he no longer has time to maneuver the ferry.

3. *Caught off Guard*. Wren is on guard duty in a combat zone. There is real danger, but the night is quiet. Lulled by the sound of the wind in the leaves, Wren has twice caught herself dozing and shaken herself awake. The third time she does not catch herself. She falls into a deep slumber, leaving the compound unguarded.

In each of these cases, the agent would definitely be blamed and might well be liable to punishment. However, when Alessandra enters the school, she does not choose to forget her obligations but is distracted from them; when Julian lapses into fantasy, he does not ignore the looming rocks but fails to notice them; and when Wren falls asleep, she does not set her duty aside but ceases to be aware of it. Thus, in each case, the difficulty appears to lie not in the agent's conscious will but in something that overtakes it.

It is of course possible to insist that being distracted, daydreaming, and falling asleep are *not* just things that happen to people—that if the wills of Alessandra, Julian, and Wren have been overtaken, it is only because they have allowed them to be. By reintroducing conscious volition at this slightly earlier point, we would in each case reestablish a locus of searchlight control that renders the agent's responsibility unproblematic. However, in so doing, we would also fly in the face of common experience. We all know what it is to be assaulted by an urgent problem that drives all other thoughts from our minds; to emerge from a reverie into which we have no recollection of choosing to enter; and to have our defenses against drowsiness infiltrated by a momentary lapse in our awareness of the need to sustain them. When such things happen, there is simply no point at which we are conscious of choosing to *allow* them to happen. Thus, if someone were to assert that all such failures of attention are nevertheless voluntary, his claim would be implausible on its face. That claim, if not backed by some powerful independent argument—and I know of none that supports it—will not so much advance our understanding of the problem as simply define it out of existence.

II

Involuntary lapses of attention, though common, do not account for the majority of the wrong acts for which we hold agents responsible. Hence, if those lapses were the only counterexamples to the thesis that responsibility presupposes searchlight control, then we could preserve that thesis by simply redrawing the boundary between responsible and nonresponsible agency. This would compel us to withdraw our judgment that agents such as Alessandra, Julian, and Wren are responsible, but would leave the majority of our current attributions of responsibility intact.

But, as I have suggested, involuntary lapses of attention are *not* the only counterexamples to the thesis that responsibility presupposes searchlight control. No less threatening, and considerably more common, are cases in which agents act wrongly because they display poor judgment. Here again are some representative examples.

4. *Home for the Holidays*. Joliet, who is afraid of burglars, is alone in the house. Panicked by sounds of movement in her kitchen, she grabs her husband's gun, tiptoes down the stairs, and shoots the intruder. It is her son, who has come home early for the holidays.

5. *Colicky Baby*. Scout, a young woman of twenty-three, has been left in charge of her sister's baby. The infant is experiencing digestive pains and has cried steadily for hours. Scout has made various attempts to ease its discomfort, but nothing has worked. Finally, to make the child sleep, she mixes vodka with its fruit juice. The child is rushed to the hospital with alcohol poisoning.

6. *Jackknife*. Father Poteet, a good driver, is gathering speed to enter a busy freeway. Because the merge lane is very short, he must either pull in front of a looming eighteen-wheeler or stop abruptly. He makes the split-second decision that he has room to merge, but he is wrong. The trucker hits the brakes hard, his truck jackknifes across four lanes of traffic, and many people are seriously injured.

In these as in our earlier examples, all three agents would definitely be blamed and might well be liable to punishment. Also as in the previous examples, none of the current agents has chosen to do anything that he thinks is wrong, and none has chosen to harm any innocent person. Although all three agents have acted voluntarily, the harm that each one does is due not to his bad will but rather to the poor judgment that *informs* his will.

Of these three cases, the first two, at least, are textbook examples of negligence. Because they are, we may be tempted say about them what philosophers and legal theorists generally say about negligence—namely, that what determines whether the agents are responsible is not whether they *did* know that they were subjecting others to an indefensible risk of harm, but rather whether they *should* have known this (or, equivalently, whether a reasonable person *would* have known it).[2] By adopting this "reasonable person" approach, we will imply that Scout is definitely responsible for poisoning the baby, that Joliet is probably responsible for shooting her son, and that Father Poteet may well be responsible for causing the accident. Because these are intuitively the right results, the "reasonable person" approach may appear to defuse the threat that these cases pose to the searchlight view.

2. See, for example, H. L. A. Hart, *Punishment and Responsibility* (Oxford: Oxford University Press, 1968), 136–57.

But, in fact, it does not; for by taking an agent's responsibility to depend on whether a reasonable person would have known that his act was too risky to be permissible, we will in effect be conceding that an agent who is *not* in this respect reasonable may be responsible even for acts that he does *not* recognize as impermissibly risky. In conceding this, we will also be conceding that such an agent can be responsible for acting wrongly despite the fact that he has not consciously chosen to do so. However, that agents can be responsible for acting wrongly despite not having consciously chosen to do so was precisely the possibility that *Home for the Holidays*, *Colicky Baby*, and *Jackknife* were introduced to illustrate. Thus, far from defending the thesis that responsibility presupposes searchlight control against a potential set of counterexamples, the introduction of the "reasonable person" test will in effect amount to an acknowledgment that that thesis cannot *be* defended.[3]

III

So far, we have seen that many of the acts for which we hold agents responsible can be traced either to unwilled lapses in attention or to equally unwilled failures of judgment. Even by themselves, these facts would raise difficult questions about the connection between responsibility and searchlight control. However, the questions become more serious yet when we factor in a third class of counterexamples—namely, those in which the agent willingly performs an act which is in fact

---

3. In this and the preceding paragraph, I have presupposed an objective interpretation of the "reasonable person" standard—that is, one that defines the agent's situation without reference to his own beliefs or mental attributes. If instead the standard is interpreted subjectively, so that it takes the test for responsibility to be whether a reasonable person who shared some or all of the agent's beliefs and dispositions would have acted as the agent did, then it may indeed preserve the principle that responsibility presupposes control. However, because the subjective version of the standard will preserve the principle by implying that Joliet, Scout, and Father Poteet are not responsible for what they have done, it will go no distance toward showing how the principle can be reconciled with the intuition that they are responsible. For discussion of the difference between the objective and subjective interpretations, see Joshua Dressler, *Understanding Criminal Law*, 3rd edition (New York: Lexis Publishing, 2001), 131–33 and 238–39.

wrong, but whose wrongness he does not recognize because he lacks some form of moral insight or imagination. Here again are three examples.

7. *Bad Joke.* Ryland is very self-absorbed. Though not malicious, she is oblivious to the impact that her behavior will have on others. Consequently, she is bewildered and a bit hurt when her rambling anecdote about a childless couple, a handicapped person, and a financial failure is not well received by an audience that includes a childless couple, a handicapped person, and a financial failure.

8. *Bad Policy.* Sylvain, a college professor, is empathetic to a fault. He identifies readily with troubled students and freely grants their requests for opportunities to earn extra credit. Because he enters so completely into each interlocutor's perspective, he often forgets that there are other, less aggressive students who would eagerly welcome the same chance. As a result, his grading policy is inconsistent and unfair.

9. *Bad Weather.* It is 1968, and amerika (a nom de guerre) is a member of the Weather Undergound. Sensitive and conscientious as a child, amerika has been rethinking his moral beliefs. In a series of stages, he has become convinced, first, that capitalism is deeply unjust; next, that nothing short of revolution will bring change; and, finally, that the need to rectify massive injustice far outweighs the rights or interests of mere individuals. To procure funds for the Revolution, amerika takes part in a robbery in which a bank guard is killed.

Of these three agents, Ryland is too self-centered to recognize her anecdote as hurtful, Sylvain is too focused on the individual before him to realize that he is being unfair to others, and amerika has taken a disastrously wrong turn in working out the implications of his moral beliefs. Nevertheless, although none of the agents willingly acts wrongly, all three seem blameworthy and one (amerika) also deserves to be punished.

We have now encountered a total of nine cases in which agents seem responsible for wrong acts whose wrongness they did not recognize. Although the agent's lack of awareness is crucial to all nine cases, it does not always take the same form. In three cases (*Hot Dog, On the Rocks, Caught off Guard*), the agent does not even realize that he is in a situation that calls for action, while in the remaining six he does realize this but lacks an accurate appreciation of what he ought to do. In one of these six cases (*Home for the Holidays*), the agent's cognitive defect is due to a distorting emotion (panic), in two others (*Bad Joke Bad Policy*), it can be traced to his insensitivity to a morally relevant factor, and in the remaining three (*Colicky Baby, Jackknife, Bad Weather*) it is a product of unadorned poor judgment. In two of the latter cases (*Colicky Baby, Jackknife*), the defective judging occurs when the agent is assessing the facts, while in the third (*Bad Weather*), it occurs when he is thinking through his moral beliefs. Because these patterns of error are quite diverse, and because each one is instantly recognizable, the range of counterexamples to the searchlight view can already be seen to be broad.

IV

But acts that are morally wrong (or, on the positive side, morally admirable or supererogatory) are not the only ones for which we view agents as responsible. We also frequently view agents as responsible both for their foolish or imprudent choices and for acts that are especially clever or effective. Because the searchlight view is generally held to apply in these contexts no less than in contexts of immorality, the next thing to note is that each of our nine cases can easily be transformed from a counterexample to the claim that *moral* responsibility presupposes searchlight control into a counterexample to the corresponding claim about *non*moral responsibility.

To transpose each example to the key of nonmoral responsibility, we need only replace each morally wrong act with a suitably imprudent one. To effect the requisite changes, let us now suppose that the hot dog of which Alessandra loses track during the wrangle at school is not Sheba, but only a part of that evening's dinner that begins to burn and causes a kitchen fire; that the boat that Julian runs onto the rocks is not a ferry but his treasured ChrisCraft; and that what Wren sleeps through is not a period of danger to her comrades but an appointment upon which her own promotion depends. Let us suppose, further, that the person whom the panicky Joliet shoots is not her son but herself; that what Scout fails to consider is not how alcohol will affect her young niece but how she herself will be affected by ingesting the contents of her sister's pharmacopia; and that instead of cutting in front of the eighteen-wheeler, Father Poteet swerves sharply to the right and plunges into a drainage ditch. Let us suppose, finally, that Ryland is summarily fired when word of her tasteless anecdote reaches her employer; that the upshot of Sylvain's susceptibility to special pleading is a flood of other special pleaders; and that as amerika ages, his misguided beliefs about the moral insignificance of the individual are replaced by equally misguided beliefs about the spiritual benefits of self-starvation and daily colonic irrigation.

Although these changes do not eliminate the wrongness of all nine original acts—at least where Ryland and Sylvain are concerned, the original act remains the same—they do transform each case into an instance of self-inflicted harm. Moreover, in each amended case, we may assume both that the agent did not realize that what he was doing would harm him and that his failure to realize this had the same source as his failure to recognize his act's wrongness in the original example. Under these assumptions, the searchlight view will imply that none of the nine agents in the amended cases are responsible for the harms or disadvantages that have resulted from their imprudence. However, when we think carefully about these agents, we encounter a number of reactions that strongly suggest that we do consider them responsible.

One such reaction concerns the urgency of mitigating the damage the agents have done to themselves. Treating Joliet's bullet wound, Scout's drug overdose, Father Poteet's internal injuries, and amerika's damaged digestive system may be very costly and may require the use of resources (organs for transplant, sophisticated diagnostic machinery) the demand for which far outruns the supply. Even if it is agreed that all citizens should be provided with medical care, many will feel that Scout and amerika, and perhaps also Joliet and Father Poteet, should be relegated to a lower place in the queue of claimants than those who are not at all responsible for their condition. Given (what I take to be) the pervasiveness of this reaction, we evidently view these agents as responsible for their imprudently self-inflicted harms despite their failure to foresee those harms.

And, along similar lines, I suspect that many would be less willing to make personal sacrifices, and would be willing to make fewer such sacrifices, to help agents like Julian, Wren, and Sylvain than to help others with identical needs but different histories. Are we as willing to wade into rocky water to retrieve a boat that was breached because its owner was not paying attention as we are to retrieve a boat that was damaged by a violent sudden storm? Would we be as ready to make a special trip to meet with someone who slept through an appointment as we would to meet with someone whose car broke down? Are we as willing to do part of the work of a colleague who is swamped because he didn't think things through as we are to do the work of someone who was incapacitated by illness? If, as I suspect, the answer in each case is "no," then the reason is again that we regard the first member of each pair, but not the second, as responsible for his own predicament.

Although these reactions suggest that we regard the majority of the agents in our amended cases as responsible, we may not have the reactions about all nine cases. To cite what look like the two most refractory examples, I would expect many to feel that Father Poteet has as strong a claim to be provided with scarce medical resources as anyone else and that helping Alessandra is no different from helping someone whose kitchen caught fire because the wiring was faulty. Yet even if we do view Father Poteet and Alessandra as having strong claims to be helped, I think most of us would also feel that Father Poteet has good reason to reproach himself for his poor judgment and that Alessandra has good reason to reproach herself for forgetting what was on the stove. In this crucial respect, Father Poteet remains very different from a driver whose injuries are due to mechanical failure or a fainting spell and Alessandra remains very different from someone whose kitchen caught fire because the wiring was faulty. Thus, even in the most problematic of our cases, our reactions suggest that we regard the agents as responsible for the self-inflicted harms that they failed to foresee.

V

Even when they are expanded to encompass acts that are imprudent as well as wrong, my nine examples remain a very limited sample of the types of cases in which we take agents to be responsible. For this reason, there may still be questions about how commonly we are willing to hold agents responsible for acts of whose wrongness or foolishness they are not aware. To bring out the pervasiveness of this phenomenon, I want next to call attention to some of the ways in which the examples can be generalized.

It should be clear, first, that each type of failure that I have mentioned—forgetting, bad judgment, insensitivity—can have many different causes and can take many different forms. To cite just a few possibilities, a person may fail to realize that he has a certain obligation (to return a phone call, look into the causes of his child's bad grades, break a piece of bad news tactfully) because his head is abuzz with information, because he finds it unpleasant to think about the situation that is generating the obligation, because he is preoccupied with his team's playoff chances, or for any number of other reasons. A person may fail to plan prudently, or may fail to see how to execute his well-wrought plan, because he is in a hurry or overeager to please, because he is worried about letting a golden opportunity slip through his fingers, or simply because he is not good at this sort of thing. A person's moral or prudential judgment may be clouded by anxiety, exhilaration, depression, anger, grief, or any other strong emotion. A person's thinking may be so rigid and stereotyped that the natural thing to do, or a tactful or rhetorically effective way of saying what must be said, just does not occur to him. And each such pattern can itself interact with any of the others, as when an agent's unwilled lapse of attention is itself what leads him to judge poorly or to fail to recognize a morally relevant consideration. For each of the possibilities just listed, we can easily tell many stories that would lead most people to judge that the agent is responsible for the ensuing wrong or foolish act.

So far, I have concentrated on cases in which agents seem responsible for acts whose morally or prudentially relevant features they do not recognize. However, an even more common type of case is that in which the agent *is* aware of all the morally and prudentially relevant features of his situation, but is mistaken about their moral or prudential *weight*. A wrongdoer who underestimates the weight of a given moral consideration stands somewhere between a psychopath, who doesn't recognize that consideration as relevant at all, and an akratic, who is fully aware of its true weight but is not (or not sufficiently) moved by it. Agents of this sort are counterexamples to the searchlight view because they are responsible despite the fact that their inaccurate weighting of the reasons renders them unaware of the wrongness or foolishness of what they are doing.

Here as above, examples are easy to come by. We are all familiar with the agent who realizes that he is doing something unsavory but incorrectly takes his act to be justified by its good consequences; with the student who realizes that cheating on exams is wrong but thinks it cannot be *too* wrong if so many others are also doing it; and with the meddler who sees value in respecting another's autonomy but who too readily believes that it is more important to prevent some harm. Along similar lines, we all know people who realize that certain acts are risky, but who fail to realize that they are acting foolishly because they underestimate the importance of what they are risking, because they cannot vividly imagine certain possibilities, or because they just don't care what will happen when they are old. In these sorts of cases, even more clearly than in the others, an agent's failure to recognize the wrongness or imprudence of what he is doing is generally thought not to relieve him of responsibility for doing it.

Given the variety of contexts in which agents can be responsible despite their failure to realize that they are acting wrongly or foolishly, and given easy availability of plausible illustrations, I suspect that clear-eyed decisions to act wrongly or foolishly are actually pretty rare. However, for present purposes, I need not say anything this strong. Instead, to propel my argument forward, I need only point out that whatever the exact ratio of unwitting to witting instances of wrongdoing and foolishness within the domain of apparently responsible action, that proportion is far higher than the searchlight view can allow.[4]

VI

We have seen that agents often seem responsible for acts of whose wrongness or foolishness they were not antecedently aware. But does this really compel us to choose between rejecting the searchlight view and drastically revising our attributions of responsibility? Can't a proponent of the searchlight view somehow square the fact that none of our nine agents was aware that he was acting wrongly or self-destructively with the intuition that each agent is responsible for what he did?

---

4. Although Michael J. Zimmerman is dealing with only a relatively narrow range of cases, he draws a conclusion of just this sort when he writes that "the conditions [for culpable ignorance] are pretty restrictive," and that therefore "culpable ignorance occurs less frequently, perhaps far less frequently, than is commonly supposed." (Michael J. Zimmerman, "Moral Responsibility and Ignorance," *Ethics* 107 [April 1997], 411). For further discussion along these lines, see Gideon Rosen, "Culpability and Ignorance," *Proceedings of the Aristotelian Society* 103 (2003), 61–83.

According to many philosophers, we can indeed achieve a recon-
ciliation by relocating each agent's conscious choice to some earlier
point in his history. If an agent previously realized that what he was then
doing would subsequently lead to his acting wrongly without realizing it
(or, less exactingly, if he realized that what he was then doing would
subsequently raise the *likelihood* of his acting wrongly without realizing
it), then his responsibility for his current wrong act may simply be a
consequence of his responsibility for his earlier one. Hence, to complete my demonstration that the searchlight view is massively incompatible with our beliefs about who is responsible for what, I must
explain why this maneuver fails. To keep things brief, I will confine
my discussion to the original versions of the nine examples. However,
everything I say will also apply, mutatis mutandis, to their nonmoral
variants.

The suggestion that what makes an agent responsible for an unwitting wrongful choice is always some previous choice that was witting
as well as wrongful is already familiar. We encountered a version of
it when we asked whether Alessandra had chosen to allow herself to
be distracted, whether Julian had chosen to daydream, and whether
Wren had chosen to let herself fall asleep. In this initial version, the
suggestion was found not to be credible. However, even if we cannot
locate the fateful choice at the moment immediately before the agent
becomes incapable of recognizing his act as wrong, we may still be able
to locate it at some yet earlier moment.

Interestingly, proposals of this sort can be extracted from two quite
different bodies of literature. One, predictably, is the literature on
culpable ignorance. It is often said that a necessary (though not a
sufficient) condition for culpability for an act that one does not recognize as wrong is the prior wrongful performance of what Holly Smith
has called a "benighting act"—that is, an act in which the agent "fails to
improve (or positively impairs) his cognitive position"[5] in a way that
creates a risk of precisely the type of wrongdoing that later occurs.
Taking our cue from this, we might suppose that the wrongful choices
that render the agents in our examples responsible consist precisely of

---

5. Holly Smith, "Culpable Ignorance," *The Philosophical Review*, 92 (October 1983),
547; see also Zimmerman, "Moral Responsibility and Ignorance."

such benighting acts. The other body of literature that might be adapted to provide a way of relocating the moment of knowing wrongful choice is the literature on character formation. Inspired by Aristotle, many philosophers have pointed out that we are at least to some extent able to shape our characters—that, among other things, we become good by practicing virtue and avoiding vice, bad by doing the reverse.[6] This suggests that the wrongful choices that have rendered our agents responsible may be those through which they solidified the habits that subsequently prevented them from realizing that what they were doing was wrong.

Because there are always innumerable past acts and omissions but for which a wrongdoer would *not* have failed to realize that he was not acting as he should, each of these proposals has some initial credibility. However, problems emerge as soon as we try to flesh the proposals out. One obvious problem is that in the majority of our nine examples, the agent's lack of awareness that he is acting wrongly simply does not appear to be traceable to any prior wrongful act or omission. A further problem is that even where there has been previous wrongdoing, the agent's responsibility does not appear to depend on his previously having been *aware* that he was acting wrongly. For ease of exposition, I will develop these objections first as they pertain to wrongful benighting acts and then as they pertain to wrongful failures to develop good habits and traits.

Have the agents in our examples knowingly and willingly performed wrongful benighting acts? To see that the majority have not, we need only remind ourselves of how unpredictable their situations were. For example, when Alessandra arrived at the school, the dispute that she encountered was not one that she could have anticipated. Because she had no previous reason to expect to be distracted, she

---

6. For relevant discussion, see Jonathan Jacobs, *Choosing Character: Responsibility for Virtue and Vice* (Ithaca: Cornell University Press, 2001); Gregory Trianosky, "Natural Affection and Responsibility for Character: A Critique of Kantian Views of the Virtues," in Owen Flanagan and Amelie Oksenberg Rorty, eds., *Identity, Character, and Morality* (Cambridge, MA: Bradford, 1990), 93–109, and Gary Watson, "Skepticism About Weakness of Will," in his *Agency and Answerability: Selected Essays* (Oxford: Oxford University Press, 2004), 33–58.

also had no previous reason to take precautions *against* being distracted. Thus, on the most natural reconstruction of *Hot Dog*, there was no previous point at which Alessandra negligently failed to do something that would have prevented her from forgetting Sheba. Nor, similarly, does the most natural reconstruction of *Jackknife* involve any wrongful benighting act on Father Poteet's part; for because he had no reason to mistrust his judgment, he also had no previous reason to take precautions against its failing. And, although I shall not bother to argue the point, I think we would be just as hard-pressed to attribute wrongful benighting acts to Julian in *On the Rocks*, to Wren in *Caught off Guard*, or to amerika in *Bad Weather.*[7]

The other four examples are different. It is clear enough that Joliet should have investigated before shooting the intruder and that Scout should have tried to find out whether babies can tolerate alcohol. It may also be true that Ryland should have stopped to think before telling her anecdote and that Sylvain should have reflected before agreeing to allow his student to earn extra credit. Hence, when it comes to these cases, the attempt to relocate the moral lapse does have some initial credibility.

However, even if all four unwitting wrong acts *can* be traced to previous wrongful benighting acts, it does not follow, nor is it plausible to say, that any of these agents must have recognized the previous act *as* either benighting or wrongful. Given Joliet's panic, it seems unlikely

---

7. For a further illustration of the problems associated with this approach, consider a case that is introduced by Eugene Schlossberger in his book *Moral Responsibility and Persons* (Philadelphia: Temple University Press, 1992). Schlossberger asks us to consider Joel, an American in England who causes a traffic accident because he does not realize that the British drive on the left. To explain why Joel is responsible for causing the accident, Schlossberger writes that "other things being equal, Joel is responsible for instantiating the trait of not having bothered to check the local traffic laws before driving. . . . For had he placed more importance on [the safety of other motorists], he would have thought that the risk to their safety, though, as far as he knew, rather slight, outweighed the extra three minutes of sleep he gained by not getting up earlier to look up the law, to make sure that no curious but important feature of English traffic laws escaped his attention" (109). This passage is both typical of what those who wish to associate all instances of culpable ignorance with prior benighting acts must do and so far-fetched that it nicely illustrates the reasons for not adopting their strategy.

that she even thought of investigating the identity of the intruder, much less realized that she was acting wrongly by not doing so. Nevertheless, even if she never was aware that she was not acting as she should, she remains responsible for shooting her son. Mutatis mutandis, the same is true of Scout in *Colicky Baby*, of Ryland in *Bad Joke*, and of Sylvain in *Bad Policy*. Thus, even if we assume that each agent did previously perform a wrongful benighting act, the four cases will remain counter-examples to the claim that agents are not responsible for their unwitting wrong acts unless those acts can be traced to previous benighting acts which in their turn were witting as well as wrongful.

So far, I have argued only that we cannot accommodate our intuitions about the nine cases by saying that what each agent is really responsible for is an earlier wrongful benighting act. But neither, similarly, can we accommodate those intuitions by saying that what each agent is really responsible for is an earlier wrongful failure to cultivate habits or traits that would subsequently have *prevented* him from acting wrongly. This suggestion, too, fails partly because most of our cases are best interpreted as involving no such failures and partly because even the remaining cases do not compel us to assume that the relevant failures were witting as well as wrongful.

To see that the majority of our cases involve no previous wrongful failures to cultivate good habits and traits, we must note, first, that agents are at best obligated to prevent the development of habits and traits that are markedly worse than normal. We may indeed act wrongly when we allow ourselves to develop vices, but we do not act wrongly by not trying to become moral saints. This is significant because in the majority of our examples, the relevant wrongful acts are *not* best understood as stemming from habits or traits that are markedly worse than normal. There is no particular reason to suppose that Alessandra, Wren, and Julian are any more irresponsible than the average person or that Joliet and Father Poteet are unusually indifferent to the safety of others. Because we need not suppose that any of these agents has been remiss in not developing his character, we draw a blank when we look for wrongfully foregone opportunities for self-improvement in which to locate their responsibility for their later wrong acts. Should Alessandra have been taking Gingko Biloba to improve her memory? Was Father Poteet remiss in not sharpening his reflexes on video games? Should Joliet have been on Paxil?

Here again, the remaining cases are different. As described, Scout sounds unusually irresponsible, Ryland sounds unusually insensitive, Sylvain sounds like he lacks a basic sense of fairness, and amerika sounds like he has lost his moral compass. Hence, in *Colicky Baby, Bad Joke, Bad Policy,* and *Bad Weather,* there is at least theoretical room for the claim that what the agent is really responsible for is wrongfully having allowed himself to develop the vice that his unwitting wrong act manifests.

Yet even if we waive the objection that each incipient vice was itself a barrier to the agent's recognition of the need to take steps to prevent its further development—the objection that, for example, the very self-involvement that now makes Ryland so insensitive is also likely to have made her unaware of the need for sensitivity training—this strategy for relocating what the agents are really responsible for will remain far-fetched. The basic problem is the relation between the way a person lives and the character he will end up having is generally transparent only in retrospect. Our characters develop slowly and by accretion, and their development is influenced not only by the decisions we make and the situations into which we enter, but also by our innate tendencies and the innumerable unchosen exigencies with which life presents us. Given the complexity of each factor, and given the exponentially greater complexity of the ways in which the different factors can inter-act, we rarely make decisions with the clear understanding that they will cause us to acquire traits or habits that are markedly worse than normal.[8] Although there may be a handful of activities that can be predicted to have such effects—working in a missile silo and being a prison guard are two that come to mind[9]—our view of the future is usually too clouded to license such inferences. We generally have little idea of which traits we will develop if we do or do not marry a certain person, undertake a certain career, or put down roots in a certain part of

8. For additional defense of the view that we rarely have an unobstructed view of the ways in which our present actions will affect our future characters, see Nomy Arpaly, *Unprincipled Virtue: An Inquiry into Moral Agency* (Oxford: Oxford University Press, 2003), 139–44.

9. For an interesting discussion of the role of character in decisions to implement nuclear threats, see Gregory Kavka, "Some Paradoxes of Deterrence," *The Journal of Philosophy* 75 (June 1978), 285–302.

the country. A fortiori, we are generally not in a position to appreciate the cumulative effects of the innumerable smaller decisions of which our daily lives consist. Thus, even if we grant that Ryland, Scout, Sylvain, and amerika were remiss in not taking what in retrospect can be recognized as the steps that were necessary to prevent the development of their current bad traits, it will remain implausible to suppose that their wrongful failures to take those steps were themselves witting.[10]

10. For further criticism of the "tracing" approach to responsibility in cases of ignorance or lack of control, see Manuel Vargas, "The Trouble With Tracing," *Midwest Studies in Philosophy* 29 (2005), 269–91; Angela Smith, "Responsibility for Attitudes: Activity and Passivity in Mental Life," *Ethics* 115 (January 2005), 236–71; and Michael McKenna, "Putting the Lie on the Control Condition for Moral Responsibility," *Philosophical Studies* 139, 29–37. In their recent Essay "The Truth About Tracing" (*Nous*, forthcoming), John Martin Fischer and Neal Tognazzini defend the tracing approach against a variety of counterexamples proposed by these authors.

THREE

RESPONSIBILITY AND PRACTICAL
REASON

IN THE PREVIOUS CHAPTER, I ARGUED THAT TAKING THE SEARCHLIGHT
view seriously would mean revising many of our judgments about who
is responsible for what. This does not compel us to reject the searchlight
view—the history of thought is littered with plausible-seeming judgments that turned out to be false—but it does imply that we should
only accept the view if the case for doing so is stronger than the case for
retaining our current judgments. Thus, the natural next question is
what can be said in favor of the searchlight view. Unfortunately, that
question is not at all easy to answer; for although the searchlight view is
implicit in much that philosophers say, it has received strikingly little
direct attention. Thus, to evaluate the case for accepting it, I will have to
engage in some imaginative reconstruction.

I

Let us begin by asking why anyone should find the searchlight view
attractive. It owes its appeal, I think, to the fact that the limits of what
it takes each agent to be responsible for are a precise match with what each
of us sees as the limits of his own choice situation when he confronts
the world *as* an agent. When we engage with the world in this way—when
we ask ourselves what we should do, weigh the reasons for and against the

acts we see as available, make our decisions on the basis of our assessment of these reasons, and so on—the process as we encounter it is at every stage fully conscious. We can only deliberate about the possibilities as we see them, can only weigh the significance of the facts as we know them, and can only base our decisions on our reasons as we understand them. Because deliberation is conscious through and through, anyone who engages in it—that is, each of us, all the time—must encounter himself simply as a (volitionally effective) center of consciousness. Even if we are aware that we hold many beliefs of which we are not aware, we must view those beliefs as inaccessible to us and hence as irrelevant to the practical question we are trying to answer.

Taken by itself, this is not an argument for the searchlight view. It is one thing to invoke the deliberative perspective to account for the searchlight view's attractiveness and quite another to invoke the deliberative perspective to *justify* the searchlight view. Still, if the searchlight view can in fact be justified, it will be surprising if its rationale does not bear some close resemblance to the main source of its appeal. Thus, in what follows, I will adopt as my working hypothesis the assumption that the best defense of the searchlight view is likely to involve some premise that makes essential mention of the deliberative perspective.

What form, exactly, might such a defense take? To answer this question, we must somehow connect the deliberative perspective to the concept of responsibility; and the most straightforward way to do this is to exploit the Kantian insight that all deliberation takes place "under the aspect of freedom." According to Kant, even if everything we do is already determined, we are incapable of thinking of ourselves as incapable of making a difference when we deliberate. In Kant's own words,

> we cannot possibly conceive of a reason as being consciously directed from outside in regard to its judgments; for in that case the subject would attribute the determination of his power of judgment, not to his reason, but to an impulse. Reason must look upon itself as the author of its own principles independently of alien influences. There-fore as practical reason, or as the will of a rational being, it must be regarded by itself as free.[1]

---

1. Immanuel Kant, *Groundwork of the Metaphysics of Morals*, trans. H. J. Paton (New York: Harper & Row, 1964), 116.

Taking their cue from this, some contemporary philosophers have claimed that the concept of responsibility has its origins, or is somehow implicit, in the very stance that we occupy when we try to decide what we should do.

That claim, if correct, is potentially relevant to our concerns; for if responsibility is indeed a practical concept, then the conditions for its application may reflect its practical origins. More specifically, because all practical deliberation takes place at the conscious level, the premise that responsibility is a practical concept may support the conclusion that the only features of their actions for which agents can be responsible are features of which they were aware when they acted. If this reasoning is sound, then the practical origins of the concept of responsibility will provide the needed bridge from the premise that deliberation is a conscious activity to the conclusion that agents are only responsible for those features of their acts of which they were consciously aware.

But *is* the reasoning sound? Can we really link our ordinary concept of responsibility this closely to practical deliberation? And, even if we can, does it really follow that the concept's application is restricted to those features of a person's acts of which he was antecedently aware? To answer these questions, we must clarify both the meaning and the implications of the claim that responsibility is a practical concept. To that task, I now turn.

II

In recent years, the claim that responsibility is a concept of practical rather than theoretical reason has been advanced by both Christine Korsgaard and Hilary Bok. In her important essay "Creating the Kingdom of Ends," Korsgaard wrote that

> [o]n Kant's view, we first encounter the idea of freedom when we are deciding what to do. We encounter it in the necessity of acting under the idea of freedom, and in the commands of the moral law. At the moment of decision, you must regard yourself as the author of your action, and so you inevitably hold yourself responsible for what you do.[2]

2. Christine Korsgaard, *Creating the Kingdom of Ends* (Cambridge: Cambridge University Press, 1996), 206.

And, along similar lines, Bok has written that

> I have argued that when we engage in practical reasoning we must
> regard ourselves not as caused to choose by antecedent events but as
> determining our conduct for ourselves...And I have argued that this
> gives us reason to regard ourselves as responsible for our conduct in a
> sense that transcends causal responsibility.[3]

Although the details of their accounts differ, Korsgaard and Bok both
deny that the point of regarding someone as responsible is either to
describe him or to explain what he has done. In Korsgaard's words, we
should not "think that it is a fact about a person that she is responsible
for a particular action."[4] Instead, both philosophers construe our attributions of responsibility as ineliminable components of our attempts to
decide what we have reason *to* do.

This way of thinking about responsibility offers some definite advantages. For one thing, by taking the concept to originate in the requirements of practical reason, we would locate it squarely within the larger
family of moral concepts (right, wrong, ought, etc.) each other member of
which is also action-guiding. Conversely, by denying that responsibility is
a property that an agent can either have or lack, we would open up the
possibility of circumventing the seemingly endless dispute about whether
the conditions for having the relevant property include not having been
caused to act. However, for present purposes, the crucial fact about the
practical approach is neither that it promises to simplify moral theory nor
that it offers a fresh perspective on the free will problem, but rather that
introducing it puts us in a position to formulate a simple argument for the
searchlight view—one that I suspect has exerted a good deal of covert
influence. Here, in brief, is how that argument runs.

3. Hilary Bok, *Freedom and Responsibility* (Princeton: Princeton University Press,
1998), 162.
4. Korsgaard, "Creating the Kingdom of Ends," 197; compare Bok: "I do not see the
distinction between the theoretical and practical points of view as a distinction between
two standpoints that allow us to describe the world in different idioms," *Freedom and
Responsibility*, 59. However, for an argument that the practical standpoint does have
explanatory (and thus theoretical) implications, see R. Jay Wallace, "Responsibility and
the Practical Point of View," sec. IV, in Ton van den Beld, ed., *Moral Responsibility and
Ontology* (Dordrecht, Holland: Kluwer, 2000), 25–47.

When we deliberate, we are attempting to decide not what is true, but rather what we should do. Because what we should do depends on the strength of the reasons for and against various possible acts, we cannot deliberate without asking ourselves whether, and if so how strongly, the different features of the acts that are available to us tell for or against their performance. However, in order to ask ourselves this question about any feature of any act, we must be thinking both about the act itself and about the feature of it that is in question. We can only think about the act if we are aware that it is among our options and we can only think about the feature if we are aware that the act would have it. Thus, from the claim that "our reasons for using [the concept of responsibility] are derived from its role in our deliberation,"[5] it may indeed seem to follow that we can be responsible only for those features of our acts of which we are antecedently aware.

In calling attention to this argument for the searchlight view, I do not wish to suggest that it is one that either Korsgaard or Bok has actually advanced. As we will see, there are indications that Korsgaard would not accept the searchlight view, while Bok's views on the matter are simply unclear. Still, if we identify our ordinary concept of responsibility with the one that we apply when we deliberate—an identification that Korsgaard and Bok both seem to endorse—then we will be hard-pressed to resist the argument's force. Thus, to assess the argument's strength, we will have to look more carefully at that identification.

Despite its initial appeal, I think the claim that our ordinary concept of responsibility is practical is deeply problematic. Put most simply, the central problem is that whereas it is logically impossible to deliberate about anything except one's own future actions, our ordinary concept of responsibility is neither oriented to the future nor restricted to the first person. That our ordinary concept of responsibility is not oriented to the future is evident from the fact that the reactions that presuppose that agents are responsible—most saliently, praise, blame, punishment, and reward—are thought to be appropriate only when the acts that occasion them are already completed and thus in the past. That our ordinary concept of responsibility is not restricted to the first person is evident from the fact that the reactions that presuppose its

5. Bok, *Freedom and Responsibility*, 146.

applicability are usually not reflexive—that our praise, blame, and the rest are most often directed not at ourselves but at other people. Because our ordinary concept of responsibility appears so different from the one that is implicit in our deliberations, the claim that these concepts are the same is implausible on its face.

This, of course, is hardly the end of the story. Although Korsgaard is happy enough to downplay the connections between responsibility and praise and blame—"[t]here is," she writes, "something obviously unattractive about taking the assessment of others as the starting point in moral philosophy"[6]—both she and Bok are well aware that those connections exist and therefore must somehow be accounted for. Moreover, each in her own way attempts to do just that. Thus, before we can assess the prospects for grounding the searchlight view in the claim that responsibility is a practical concept, we will have to examine the ways in which Korsgaard and Bok have tried to show that a practical concept of responsibility can apply not only to our own future acts, but also to (a) acts that we have already performed and (b) the acts of others.

III

If practical reason is exclusively future-oriented, then how can the concept of responsibility to which it gives rise apply to past as well as future acts? Although Korsgaard and Bok agree that the concept of responsibility is practical, they appeal to very different features of practical reason to show that the concept's sphere of application encompasses past acts. Here, in brief, is what each has said.

Where Korsgaard is concerned, the crucial feature of practical reason is its mutual or reciprocal quality, and the reason this feature is crucial is that genuine mutuality can obtain only among temporally enduring agents. That this is Korsgaard's position is suggested by the combination of her well-known insistence that "the only reasons that are possible are the reasons we can share"[7] and her contention that "you cannot enter into *any* reciprocal relations . . . if you do not take

---

6. Korsgaard, "Creating the Kingdom of Ends," 189.
7. Korsgaard, "Creating the Kingdom of Ends," 301.

responsibility for your own actions at other times, since relationships after all are enduring things."[8] It is suggested, more concretely, by her illustrative treatment of Parfit's Russian nobleman example. In that example, a young socialist who intends to distribute his inheritance to the poor when he receives it, but who fears that he may become conservative and change his mind before then, attempts to preempt the change by asking his wife to hold him to his current promise to redistribute.[9] By thus dissociating himself from the decisions of his future self, Korsgaard argues, the young nobleman is both disavowing his own future agency and, in so doing, depriving his wife of the sort of temporally extended partner that genuine collaborative decision-making requires. As Korsgaard herself puts it,

> [t]he young nobleman's attitude toward his own future attitudes is essentially a *predictive* and theoretical one, and, because it is so, he abdicates the kind of responsibility that is necessary for reciprocity: the kind of responsibility that enables people to act in concert.[10]

Although the example as cited concerns only the nobleman's refusal to take responsibility for his own *future* actions, Korsgaard presumably views her argument as bidirectional. She would presumably maintain that in order to be the sorts of agents with whom others can act in concert, we must be willing to take responsibility for what we have done no less than for what we expect to do.

Korsgaard's implied argument that our practical concept of responsibility applies to what we have already done is part of her larger interpersonal theory of practical reason. By contrast, Bok's argument for the same thesis is much more narrowly focused. In her view, the practical considerations that compel us to view ourselves as responsible for what we have done pertain not to our ability to deliberate in concert with others but only to the adequacy of our own future decisions.

According to Bok, the way our past acts bear on our future decisions is by disclosing enduring features of our characters that are likely to

8. Korsgaard, "Creating the Kingdom of Ends, " 207; emphasis in orginal.

9. See Derek Parfit, "Later Selves and Moral Principles," in Alan Montefiore, ed., *Philosophy and Personal Relations* (London: Routledge and Kegan Paul, 1973), 145–46.

10. Korsgaard, "Creating the Kingdom of Ends"; emphasis in original.

influence those decisions. For example, if I have acted cruelly or dishonestly in the past, then the cruel or dishonest streak that I then manifested may well lead me to act cruelly or dishonestly again in the future. Thus, if I accept a set of practical principles that forbid cruelty and dishonesty, then the reasons these principles give me not to act in these ways are also reasons to change these aspects of my character. Moreover, since I cannot know whether I have reason to alter my character without knowing whether my past acts *have* violated my practical principles, the same principles also give me reason to reflect on my past acts and omissions (including those that caused or allowed my character to develop as it did) with an eye to discovering what I should have done differently. Thus, insofar as we occupy the practical stance, Bok concludes that each of us has "reason to define and to use a conception of responsibility according to which we are responsible for those actions that reveal the quality of our character and our will."[11]

Given the complexity of these arguments, we obviously cannot evaluate either philosopher's position without addressing various further questions. To assess Korsgaard's account, we would have to ask how practical reason can be essentially interpersonal if its core question— what should I do?—is one that each individual must answer for himself. We would also have to ask exactly how Korsgaard's remarks about the Russian nobleman can be applied to his past as opposed to his future choices. To assess Bok's account, we would have to ask, among other things, whether our attempts to identify and alter the character flaws that our past acts manifested are either backward-looking enough or focused enough on the acts themselves to qualify as taking responsibility for those acts. Although I have addressed some of these issues elsewhere,[12] any full treatment would obviously take us far afield.

But, fortunately, no such treatment is needed here. Put most simply, the reason we can afford to sidestep a closer examination of Korsgaard's and Bok's accounts is that even if both philosophers have succeeded in showing that a practical concept of responsibility must

---

11. Bok, *"Freedom and Responsibility,"* 139.

12. For an extended discussion of the relation between a bad act and the character of the person who performs it, see chapters 2 and 3 of my book *In Praise of Blame* (New York: Oxford University Press, 2006).

apply to past as well as future acts,[13] the premises upon which they base this conclusion are not ones that can be pressed into service to support an omnitemporal version of the searchlight view. We were able to derive a forward-looking version of the searchlight view from the premise that we must regard ourselves as responsible when we deliberate because we can only deliberate about those features of the available acts of which we are currently aware. However, when we think of those same acts afterwards, we often recognize facts about them of which we were *not* antecedently aware. Moreover, when Korsgaard and Bok argue that practical reason also compels us to take responsibility for our actions after we perform them, the aspects of practical reason to which they appeal provide no reason to disregard these newly appreciated facts. If the reason we must take responsibility for what we have done is either to sustain relations of mutuality with others or to avoid future betrayals of our own principles, then the limits of what we must take responsibility for appear to be set not by what we realized when we acted but rather by what we realize now. Thus, even if Korsgaard and Bok are correct in maintaining that we must regard ourselves as responsible in retrospect as well as in prospect, their arguments do not appear to show that the features of our actions for which we must take retrospective responsibility are restricted to those of which we were prospectively aware.

To bring this point into sharper focus, let me briefly elaborate it as it applies to each philosopher's reasoning. Where Korsgaard is concerned, the argument was that practical reason requires a form of mutuality that can only exist among temporally extended agents, and that therefore compels us to take responsibility for our past as well as our future acts. At least offhand, there is nothing in this mutuality requirement that restricts the features of our past acts for which we must take responsibility to features of which we were antecedently aware. Indeed, if anything, the prospects for mutuality are actually enhanced when we take responsibility for a more extensive range of features of our past acts. Suppose, for example, that when the Russian nobleman was young, he was so obsessed with social justice that he was blind to the need to hold on to some of his money to provide for his children. If this is how things were, then the nobleman and his wife will obviously be in a better position to weigh

---

13. They can both succeed in showing this because their arguments are different but not incompatible.

the relevant considerations together if he subsequently recognizes and takes responsibility for his earlier omissions. Thus, if taking responsibility for what one has done is a prerequisite for codeliberation, then the features of one's past acts for which one must take responsibility can hardly be restricted to those of which one was antecedently aware.

An analogous point can be made about Bok's argument. Even if we accept her claim that anyone who accepts a set of practical principles must scrutinize his previous actions for evidence of character defects that might prevent him from acting on those principles in the future, there is nothing in this requirement that restricts anyone's investigation to those features of his past acts of which he was antecedently aware. Indeed, if anything, our ability to minimize future violations of our principles seems again to be enhanced by our willingness to own up to the bad features of our acts of which we were previously *un*aware. Thus, to stick with our amended nobleman example, if in his youth the Russian nobleman was insufficiently attentive to the needs of his children, then the obvious first step toward improving both his character and his conduct is precisely to take responsibility for the failures to consider his children's needs that he did not previously recognize as wrong. Thus, if taking responsibility for what one has done is called for as a way of minimizing future violations of one's principles, then the features of one's past acts for which one must take responsibility are again not restricted to those of which one was antecedently aware.

IV

So far, we have seen that there are more and less expansive versions of the claim that practical reason gives rise to a concept of responsibility. In its least expansive version, which derives the concept exclusively from the demands of the deliberative perspective, the claim does seem to imply that we are responsible only for those features of our acts of which we are antecedently aware, but it does so at the cost of restricting our responsibility to acts that we have not yet performed. By contrast, in its more expansive versions, each of which relies on some richer notion of practical reason, the claim does *not* restrict our responsibility to acts that we have not yet performed, but it also does not preserve the implication that we are responsible only for those features of our acts of which we are antecedently aware. Because we have found no version of the practical approach that yields a concept of responsibility that is both backward- as well as forward-looking and restricted to the features of our acts of which we are antecedently aware, we have also found no version that supports the claim that our ordinary concept of responsibility (which undeniably *is* backward- as well as forward-looking) presupposes searchlight control.

Even by itself, this objection seems strong enough to discredit the inference from the premise that our ordinary concept of responsibility is practical to the conclusion that that concept presupposes the searchlight view. However, that inference becomes still more problematic when we shift our focus from the claim that practical reason yields a concept of responsibility that applies to our own past acts to the claim that practical reason yields a concept of responsibility that applies to the acts of others. Because the exact nature of the problem will vary with the reasons for thinking that a practical concept of responsibility must apply to the acts of others, and because Korsgaard and Bok defend this claim in very different ways, I will again discuss their arguments separately.

In Korsgaard's view, the way in which practical reason compels us to view others as responsible for their acts is by compelling us to enter into relations of reciprocity with them. Reciprocity, which Korsgaard takes to lie at the heart of both moral and personal relationships, requires both that we view other people's ends as reasons because they seek them and that we expect the others to view our own ends as reasons because *we* seek them. These requirements give us reason to regard other people as just as capable of weighing reasons, and hence as just as responsible for any ensuing decisions, as we ourselves are:

> The relations of reciprocity . . . call for mutual responsibility for two important reasons. In order to make the ends and reasons of another your own, you must regard her as a source of value, someone whose choices confer worth upon their objects, and who has a right to decide on her own actions. In order to entrust your own ends and reasons to another's care, you must suppose that she regards you that way, and is prepared to act accordingly. . . . Reciprocity is the sharing of reasons, and you will enter into it only with someone you expect to deal with reasons in a rational way. In this sense, reciprocity requires that you hold the other responsible.[14]

14. Korsgaard, "Creating the Kingdom of Ends," 196.

Because practical reason requires a form of reciprocity that can only exist among beings each of whom views himself as only one rational agent among others, any practical concept of responsibility will have to be intersubjective as well as transtemporal.

Like Korsgaard's argument that the practical concept of responsibility must apply to past as well as future acts, her argument that it must apply to others as well as ourselves gives rise to many further questions. They are, indeed, many of the same questions. However, also as with Korsgaard's previous argument, we need not answer these questions to see that the current argument for extending the practical concept of responsibility to others does not preserve the implication that those others are responsible only for those features of their acts of which they were antecedently aware.

Put most simply, the reason the current argument does not preserve this implication is that it treats responsibility only as a general capacity. What it says is only that in order to enter into relations of reciprocity with others, we must regard them as responsible in the sense of having the capacity to deliberate about what they have reason to do, and of having the further capacity to take our own deliberative capacity into account when they do so. Because regarding someone as responsible in this sense has no implications at all about what we must regard him as responsible *for*, this argument goes no distance toward showing that we must view others as responsible only for those features of their acts of which they are antecedently aware. It is of course true that other people cannot regard *themselves* as responsible for any features of any available acts of which *they* are unaware; but the crucial question is precisely whether we have reason to import this limitation on the others' awareness, which is internal to *their* (part of our shared) deliberative perspective, into our own quite different point of view. Because Korsgaard's reciprocity argument gives us no such reason, it appears to be fully consistent with the view that agents can be held responsible even for those features of their acts of which they are not antecedently aware.

Indeed, there are indications that Korsgaard herself would accept this view. For one thing, she clearly thinks we have considerable discretion about when we do and do not hold others responsible. She writes, for example, that "while of course facts about the agent and about her condition at the time of the action *guide* your decision about whether to hold her responsible, they do not fully *determine* it."[15] Although she mainly emphasizes the contexts in which charity or kindness decrees that we not hold others responsible even though we might, her view also leaves us a good deal of leeway in the other direction. In addition, she explicitly acknowledges that

> we may well blame people for involuntary attitudes or expressions, because we blame people for lack of control itself. If you cannot repress a victorious grin on learning that your rival has met with a gruesome accident, you ought to be blamed, precisely on that account.[16]

Given her evident willingness to hold agents responsible for reactions that are not voluntary, it is hard to see on what basis Korsgaard could rule out holding them responsible for features of their acts over which they lack searchlight control.

Unlike Korsgaard, who bases her extension of the practical concept of responsibility to others on her views about the intersubjectivity of practical reasons, Bok bases her version of the extension on the simpler premise that we have good reason to regard others as, in the relevant ways, just like us. Bok argues, in particular, that each of us has good reason to regard others as "persons who are capable of governing their lives through practical reasoning,"[17] and that "[w]hen we regard others as persons, we must both extend to them a view we would otherwise take of ourselves and allow ourselves to enter into their view of themselves."[18] From these premises, together with her previous conclusion that practical reason compels us to view ourselves as responsible (and the further premise that each other person's practical reason can be seen to impose the same demands on him), Bok concludes that we are indeed compelled to extend our practical concept of responsibility to others as well as ourselves.

We have already seen that Bok's (and Korsgaard's) reasons for extending the practical concept of responsibility from our own future acts to our own past acts do not preserve the implication that we are responsible

---

15. Korsgaard, "Creating the Kingdom of Ends," 198.
16. Korsgaard, 198–99.
17. Bok, *Freedom and Responsibility*, 188.
18. Bok, 188.

only for the features of those acts of which we were antecedently aware. Thus, even if Bok's current argument succeeds in showing that we must view other people as responsible for their own past acts in exactly the same sense in which we are responsible for ours, it will not support the conclusion that we must view those others as responsible only for those features of their own past acts of which they were antecedently aware. However, we have also seen that it does seem plausible to say that we can only view ourselves as responsible for those features of our own *future* acts of which we are now aware. Thus, the question that remains is whether Bok's current argument can at least support the conclusion that we are similarly restricted to viewing others as responsible only for those features of *their* future acts of which they are now aware.

When we deliberate, the reason we cannot view ourselves as responsible for any features of our own potential acts of which we are unaware is, trivially, that we are not aware of those features. Thus, to mount a parallel argument that we also cannot view others as responsible for any features of their potential acts of which *they* are unaware, we would have to show that this restriction, too, follows trivially from someone's lack of awareness of those features. But from whose lack of awareness could the restriction follow trivially? It clearly cannot be a trivial consequence of *the others'* lack of awareness that the acts available to them would have the relevant features, since the only thing that follows trivially from this is a restriction on what the others can regard *themselves* as responsible for. It also cannot be a trivial consequence of *our own* lack of awareness that the acts available to the others would have the relevant features, since we, unlike them, may indeed be aware of this. Of course, we would not be aware of it if "allow[ing] ourselves to enter into [the others'] view of themselves" involved rendering ourselves unaware of everything of which they are not also aware. However, although it is indeed possible for us to *discount* some of the things of which we but not the others are aware, the actual excision of these items from our consciousness is clearly impossible. Because this is so, and because nothing less than their actual excision can support the proposed extension of our earlier argument, we may safely dismiss the suggestion that the same reasoning that previously established that we cannot view ourselves as responsible for those features of our own potential acts of which we are unaware will now support a similar restriction on our attributions of responsibility to others.

FOUR

KANTIAN FAIRNESS

SO FAR, I HAVE ARGUED THAT WE CANNOT DERIVE THE SEARCHLIGHT view from the premise that the concept of responsibility has its origins in the deliberative perspective. However, even if this argument is correct, there remains an alternative route to the searchlight view. Many of its proponents, if pressed to explain why agents are not responsible for what they did not foresee, would reply that holding them responsible is unfair because their lack of foresight deprived them of control. In the current chapter, I will examine the rationale for taking the familiar principle that it is unfair to hold agents responsible for what is beyond their control to extend to such cases. Although this discussion will lead us straight back to the deliberative perspective, the resulting indirect appeal to that perspective will turn out to be no more successful than its simpler predecessor.

I

The principle that it is unfair to hold agents responsible for what is beyond their control is compatible with many theories of rightness. It can, for example, be combined either with a theory that says we morally ought to do whatever will produce the best consequences or with one that takes an act's rightness to depend on the universalizability or rationality-respectingness of the agent's maxim. However, although the principle has no particular connection to Kant's theory of the right, it does seem connected to his theory of moral worth. It is, in particular, often thought to be the basis for his claim that an act's moral value depends entirely on the quality of the agent's will—that a good will, even if ineffective, would "shine like a jewel for its own sake."[1] To mark the principle's connection to this aspect of Kant's moral theory, I shall from now on refer to it as *The Kantian Principle*.

In its generic form, the Kantian Principle is very widely accepted. Here are three representative formulations that appear, respectively, in recent works on responsibility, free will, and moral luck.

> It is often said to be unjust to blame someone for what he could not help doing.... We think it unfair to adopt an attitude of disapproval toward someone on account of an act or omission, where this was something outside his control.[2]

> It is an illicit generalization to infer that having alternative possibilities is never required for moral responsibility or free will—throughout an entire lifetime. One could claim this only if one could claim that it is fair to hold persons responsible for being what they are even though there is nothing they could ever have done to make themselves different than they are.[3]

> If morality depends on luck, then at least sometimes people are judged morally for things that are beyond their control. This seems to be unfair; one does not deserve to be held responsible for what is beyond one's control.[4]

Although these quotations leave the terms "control" and "fairness" unanalyzed, it may seem easy enough to extract accounts of their meaning from the standard arguments for the Kantian Principle.

1. Immanuel Kant, *Groundwork of the Metaphysics of Morals*, trans. H. J. Paton (New York: Harper and Row, 1964), 62. For a statement of the view that Kant's view of moral worth reflects an ideal of fairness, see Bernard Williams, *Ethics and the Limits of Philosophy* (Cambridge, MA: Harvard University Press, 1985), 195.

2. Jonathan Glover, *Responsibility* (London: Routledge and Kegan Paul, 1970), 70, 73.

3. Robert Kane, "Responsibility, Reactive Attitudes and Free Will: Reflections on Wallace's Theory," *Philosophy and Phenomenological Research* 64 (May 2002), 697.

4. Daniel Statman, "Introduction," in Daniel Statman, ed., *Moral Luck* (Albany, NY: State University of New York Press, 1993), 2–3.

Unfortunately, this interpretive strategy is less promising than it appears; for explicit justifications of the Kantian Principle are hard to come by. Although I cannot reproduce enough of the surrounding text to document my claim, I think it is fair to say that none of the authors just quoted has even hinted at a defense that might illuminate the principle's notions of control and fairness. I also think it is fair to say that although the Kantian Principle is more often baldly asserted than carefully defended, it is even more often presupposed than explicitly stated.[5] Although the Kantian Principle is very widely accepted, it has received virtually no critical analysis or defense.

Given this dearth of argumentation, how are we to draw the line between those attributions of responsibility that the Kantian Principle does and does not condemn as unfair? How, equivalently, are we to draw the line between those cases in which agents do, and in which they do not, exercise the relevant form of control? Because responsibility is widely viewed as a prerequisite for the legitimacy of praise, blame, and punishment, and because praise, blame, and punishment are by their nature reactions to particular persons, we may plausibly dismiss as incoherent the idea that attributions of responsibility can fairly be based on facts about any individuals other than the relevant agents themselves. However, this observation, though helpful, will not settle the crucial question of whether, and if so why, the only relevant facts about an agent are those that concern his conscious choices. Why shouldn't they also include facts about the relation between his acts and his unchosen vices? About the relation between his acts and his native talents or limitations? About the relation between his acts and facts that he has learned but cannot at the moment retrieve? Because there is so much more to each agent than whatever is currently before

---

5. Interestingly, the contemporary philosopher who has paid the most attention to the Kantian Principle is R. Jay Wallace, a compatibilist. In his book *Responsibility and the Moral Sentiments* (Cambridge, MA: Harvard University Press, 1994), Wallace is admirably attentive both to the normative content of the relevant notion of fairness and to the ways in which the various excusing and exempting conditions render blame and the attribution of responsibility unfair in the relevant sense. However, even Wallace offers no real defense of the Kantian Principle: he seems more interested in the questions of what the Kantian Principle means and what it implies than in the question of why, if at all, we should accept it.

his mind, there is clearly room for a conception of control—indeed, for far more than one—that does not take it to require conscious choice.

We cannot assume that any single version of the Kantian Principle is canonical. Instead, there may be several equally defensible versions each of which interprets control and the form of fairness that requires it differently. However, to establish that the Kantian Principle supports the searchlight view, a proponent of the searchlight view need not winnow through all of its possible versions, but need only defend whichever version does take conscious awareness to be a necessary condition for control. Conversely, to rebut his argument for the searchlight view, his opponent need only establish that this version of the Kantian Principle is *not* defensible. Thus, our next task is to examine just this version of the Kantian Principle. What, exactly, does it involve, and why, if at all, should we accept it?

II

Although we cannot derive the searchlight view directly from the demands of the deliberative perspective, there remains a striking similarity between the conceptions of fairness and control that would have to inform a version of the Kantian Principle that supported the searchlight view and the way we naturally think of fairness and control whenever we take up the deliberative perspective. To bring this similarity into the open, and thus to see why the best way of defending the relevant version of the Kantian Principle is to return to the demands of the deliberative perspective, we need only remind ourselves of certain facts that have already emerged.

For, as we have already seen, the only considerations to which we can appeal when we are trying to decide what we should do are considerations that are actually before our minds. This means that when it comes to deliberation, our conscious beliefs are relevant in a way that the unconscious elements of our psychology—the beliefs and desires of which we are not aware, our abilities, dispositions, and traits, etc.—are not. Although our conscious beliefs represent only a tiny fraction of our psychological states, the fact that we are not aware of most of our other states means that they cannot enter into (although they can of course causally influence) the content of our deliberations.

From our standpoint as deliberating agents, the whole field of our unconscious attitudes and tendencies (and, I might add, the physical mechanisms that make possible both the conscious and the unconscious aspects of our mental lives) are relevant only insofar as we are conscious enough of their existence to take this into account in our deliberations.

Because the only facts to which we can appeal when we deliberate are facts of which we are aware, a deliberating agent's conscious beliefs must be central both to his conception of what is within his control and to his conception of what he may fairly be asked to do. When we deliberate, we necessarily view our control as extending only as far as the possibilities of which we are conscious. Because our aim is to reach a decision about what we should do, we cannot coherently take what is within our control to encompass either any aspect of the world that we do not see how to influence or anything that lies entirely beyond the horizon of our consciousness. Although an external observer might indeed have use for a more capacious conception of control, no such conception could match our practical aims. From our perspective as deliberating agents, the only form of control that matters is searchlight control.

And, because of this, we naturally feel that we are not being dealt with fairly when we are confronted with demands whose satisfaction requires information to which we lack conscious access. Such demands can take a number of different forms. In one type of case, the demanded outcome is clear enough ("Put out the cat before you leave") but the way to implement it is not (because, e.g., the cat hides whenever it thunders). In another, the demand is nonspecific in some crucial respect (e.g., "Meet me downtown"). In yet another, the demand is altogether unintelligible to us (as, e.g., when it is expressed in Croatian). In each case, the person who is making the demand may not be acting unreasonably: he may have no reason to believe that we will not be able to do what he says. However, even if we recognize that the person himself is not unreasonable, we will continue to think that what he is demanding is. Because we cannot see how to comply with that demand, it is, from our own perspective, quite unfair.

Can we exploit these linked conceptions of control and unfairness to arrive at a version of the Kantian Principle that is both defensible and capable of supporting the searchlight view? As a first attempt, we might simply incorporate each conception into the Kantian Principle. On the resulting account, the form of control in whose absence it is unfair to hold an agent responsible will simply be searchlight control, while the sense in which it is unfair to hold an agent responsible for a feature of an act over which he lacked searchlight control will simply be that in which he himself would have regarded as unfair a demand that he perform or not perform an act with that feature. Because the relevant senses of control and fairness seem tolerably clear, so too does the resulting version of the Kantian Principle. Moreover, because we understand what is wrong with being unreasonable, we also seem to understand this version's normative force. Thus, by interpreting the Kantian Principle's conceptions of control and fairness in this way, we may seem to have arrived at just the version of it to which proponents of the searchlight view must appeal.

III

However, before we can accept this conclusion, we must face up to an important complication: namely, that what the deliberative perspective compels an agent to *regard* as unfair is not at all the same as what the proposed version of the Kantian Principle *condemns* as unfair. When an agent deliberates, what he must regard as unfair are simply certain demands that are directed at him—demands that he cannot then see how to fulfill. By contrast, what the proposed interpretation of the Kantian Principle condemns as unfair are certain ways of reacting to an agent—most notably, blaming him in a way that implies that he is responsible—when he fails to *conform* to demands that he cannot see how to fulfill.

Because blaming or holding someone responsible for failing live up to a demand that he was bound to view as unfair is distinct from, and is logically more complex than, the demand itself, we cannot automatically infer the unfairness of the blame or attribution of responsibility from the (perceived or actual) unfairness of the demand. Worse yet, because blaming and holding people responsible are not themselves demands, the sense in which they are unfair cannot be identical to the sense in which demands seem unfair to those who cannot see how to meet them. This does not mean that no version of the Kantian Principle can incorporate a conception of unfairness that is closely related to the one that is built into the deliberative perspective; but it does mean that we cannot accept such a principle without understanding what its further conception of unfairness amounts to. Exactly why *should* holding someone responsible for failing to fulfill a demand that he was bound to view as unfair be viewed as unfair in any further sense?

The need to answer this question casts serious doubt on the proposed version of the Kantian Principle; for even if each person whom we blame or hold responsible was unable to appeal to any considerations beyond his conscious beliefs when he made his decision, there is no obvious reason for *us* to restrict our attention in this way when we consider his decision after the fact. From our retrospective and external vantage point, his conscious beliefs have no particular priority over his physical makeup or unconscious attitudes or traits. Hence, as long as blaming and holding people responsible are reactions that we have to them from a perspective that does not coincide with their own, the way they must view their choice situations when they deliberate will provide us with no obvious reason *not* to base our blame or attributions of responsibility on facts about them and their choice situations of which they were not aware.

But *are* blaming and holding people responsible really reactions that we have to them from a perspective other than their own? Thomas Nagel, for one, has suggested that they are not. In Nagel's view, blaming or holding someone responsible necessarily involves imaginatively reconstructing both the choice situation as he saw it and the reasons that he took to tell for and against each available option. Referring to the agent as the defendant and the person holding him responsible as the judge, Nagel puts the point this way:

> [I]n a judgment of responsibility the judge doesn't just decide that what has been done is a good or a bad thing, but tries to enter into the defendant's point of view as an agent. . . . he tries to assess the action in light of the alternatives presenting themselves to the defendant— among which he chose or failed to choose, and in light of the considerations and temptations bearing on the choice—which he considered or failed to consider.[6]

6. Thomas Nagel, *The View from Nowhere* (Oxford: Oxford University Press, 1986), 120.

If Nagel is right to say that we cannot blame or hold a person responsible without entering into his own point of view, then blaming or holding someone responsible may indeed compel us to share that person's conviction that any demands that he cannot see how to meet are unfair because unreasonable.

Given Nagel's assertion that a judge may take account of "considerations and temptations...which [the defendant] failed to consider," we may reasonably conjecture that Nagel himself does not view the judge's identification with the defendant as total. However, any retreat to a partial-identification view is bound to reopen a gap between the defendant's practical and forward-looking first-person perspective and the judge's evaluative and retrospective third-person perspective. For this reason, any such retreat will render problematic the inference from the premise that an agent himself must regard as unfair any demand that he cannot see how to meet to the conclusion that anyone who is tempted to blame or hold an agent responsible must take a similar view. However, it was precisely because it promised to support that inference that Nagel's proposal was introduced. Thus, for present purposes, the only version of Nagel's proposal that we need to consider is the one that takes blaming and attributing responsibility to require *full* identification.

But, whatever else is true, this version of his proposal cannot be right. It cannot be right to say that blaming or holding an agent responsible requires entering *fully* into his own point of view because if it did, then no one could identify with any (non-akratic) agent in the requisite way without regarding whatever that agent took himself to have the most reason to do as exactly what he *did* have most reason to do. Because fully adopting someone's perspective means seeing each aspect of his situation exactly as he saw it, we cannot both fully adopt a non-akratic agent's perspective and at the same time judge that he has attached too much or too little weight to some morally or prudentially relevant consideration. However, if we do *not* believe that a non-akratic agent has attached too little weight to some morally or prudentially relevant consideration—if, in other words, we do not believe that he has acted wrongly or foolishly—then there is, from the perspective that we share with him, nothing to blame him for and no wrong or foolish act for which to hold him responsible. Thus, properly understood, blame and the attribution of responsibility not only do not require full identification with the persons at whom they are directed, but actually require a degree of detachment that is incompatible with it.

IV

And so our question remains: even if agents themselves must regard as unreasonable, and thus as unfair, all demands that they cannot see how to fulfill, in what sense, and why, is it also unfair for us to blame or hold them responsible for not *fulfilling* such demands? Why, given our access to facts about them that their own perspective as agents is bound to occlude, should we not react to them in ways that reflect our superior knowledge?

To focus our thinking about this question, we may begin by noting that many reactions to a person's failure to fulfill a demand that he was bound to regard as unfair are *not* themselves unfair. It is, for example, not at all unfair to react to such an agent by feeling sorry for him; by regretting the limits on what he realized about his situation; by deciding to have nothing further to do with him; by trying to enlighten him about what he did not realize; or by making public one's belief that he did not appreciate the significance of what he was doing. Because these and many other reactions to a person's failure to live up to a demand that he would have regarded as unfair are not themselves unfair, any attempt to show that blaming and holding him responsible *are* unfair must appeal some feature that is peculiar to the latter reactions. But which of their features, if any, might bear the argument's weight?

When we compare blaming and holding responsible to the other reactions on our list, the difference that stands out is that only blaming and holding responsible commit us to *endorsing* the moral or prudential demand that we take the agent not to have satisfied. When someone acts wrongly because he is unaware of some crucial aspect of his choice situation, those who react by pitying him, by severing ties with him, or by trying to enlighten him are not thereby seconding any demand that he himself would have regarded as unfair. Whatever else is true, these reactions are all compatible with the agent's own previous view of what could reasonably be asked of him. By contrast, when someone blames or holds such an agent responsible, he implies that it *was* legitimate to demand that the agent do something other than what he did. Though of course aware that the crucial moment has passed, the person who blames or holds the agent responsible is still endorsing the unfulfilled demand as it applied to the agent *at* the crucial moment.

The fact that blame and the attribution of responsibility involve the retrospective endorsement of the demand that the agent is believed not to have met suggests a new approach to our unresolved problem. It suggests both a new way of interpreting the Kantian Principle's conception of unfairness in light of the conception implicit in the deliberative perspective—an interpretation that, if defensible, will enable the Kantian Principle to support the searchlight view—and a new way of defending the Kantian Principle as so interpreted. To complete my assessment of the prospects for grounding the searchlight view in an appropriate version of the Kantian Principle, I will discuss each aspect of this new approach.

The reason there is still a question about the Kantian Principle's conception of unfairness is that the conception implicit in the deliberative perspective—the one that takes a demand to be unfair whenever the agent at whom it is directed cannot see how to fulfill it—applies only to demands but not to any subsequent reactions to agents who fail to fulfill them. For this reason, that conception may not seem to apply to blame or the attribution of responsibility, each of which typically *is* a reaction to an agent's (perceived) failure to fulfill some moral or prudential demand. However, because retrospectively endorsing a demand is in many ways similar to making one, we may plausibly suppose that any conception of unfairness that applies to a demand itself will also apply to its retrospective endorsement. Thus, given that blaming or holding an agent responsible always does involve the retrospective endorsement of a demand that the agent is thought not to have met, the obvious way to make sense of the claim that such a reaction can be unfair is to take the reaction's unfairness to reside exclusively in its retrospective-endorsement component. By adopting this interpretation, we may hope to bridge the gap between the sense of "unfair" that pertains to demands and the sense that pertains to blame and the attribution of responsibility.

However, even if we do, there will remain a question about why we should accept the resulting version of the Kantian Principle. Why, exactly, should a conception of unfairness that has its natural home in the deliberative perspective have a normative claim on anyone who does not occupy that perspective? It is clear enough why someone who is told to do something that he does not see how to do must *himself* regard that demand as unfair, but nothing yet said explains why some other person, who does not share his perspective, must take a similar view. This last question—Why should the perspective of the agent be as authoritative for others as it is for him?—remains the central challenge to our ability to defend an interpretation of the Kantian Principle that supports the searchlight view.

But given the linkage between blaming or holding an agent responsible and retrospectively endorsing a demand that he is thought not to have fulfilled, there may indeed be a way to meet this challenge. Put most simply, the fact on which the envisioned response turns is that demands are by their nature constrained by the perspectives of those to whom they are addressed. To demand something of an agent (to ask him to do something, require something of him, etc.) is to try to influence his thinking in a way that will lead him to decide to perform the demanded act. To offer any hope of eliciting such a decision, the demand must be accessible enough to the agent to play a suitable role in his practical deliberation. This requirement is violated whenever the agent lacks some crucial item of information about what is demanded—when, for example, he cannot respond to a demand that he stop endangering his child because he is unaware that, or of how, he *is* endangering his child. Not coincidentally, these are just the conditions under which the agent himself would reject the demand as unfair because unreasonable. Thus, because no demand can achieve its aim unless it is accessible to the agent to whom it is directed, we may indeed seem entitled to conclude that the target agent's perspective is authoritative in determining which demands are unfair.[7]

This way of defending the authority of the agent's perspective bears some resemblance to the Nagelian argument that we considered above. Like the Nagelian argument, the current argument seeks to ground the

---

7. In proposing this argument, I may appear to be conflating the making of a demand by a person—a kind of illocutionary act—with the sort of demand that can be extracted from an abstract set of principles such as morality. However, the observation that no demand can achieve its aim unless it is accessible to the agent to whom it is directed appears to hold no less of the demands of morality than of demands made by particular persons.

authority of the agent's perspective in certain facts about what blaming and holding responsible are. However, unlike the Nagelian argument, the current argument bases its conclusion not on the premise that anyone who blames or holds an agent responsible must fully identify with him, but rather on the premise that anyone who blames or holds an agent responsible must endorse a demand whose initial prospects for success depended on its accessibility to that agent. Because that premise is considerably more plausible than its Nagelian counterpart, the current argument represents a definite step forward. However, it is one thing to say this, and quite another to say that the current argument succeeds in establishing a version of the Kantian Principle that supports the searchlight view.

V

And, in fact, the current argument does not succeed; for its pivotal premise—that no demand can influence an agent's deliberation unless it is accessible to him—is true only in a sense that is far too weak to establish the version of Kantian Principle that supports the searchlight view. To support the searchlight view, the Kantian Principle must assert that it is unfair to blame or hold an agent responsible for anything that he did not consciously choose. Thus, to establish this version of the Kantian Principle, the current argument's central premise must equate access with conscious awareness. It must assert that no demand can influence any agent's deliberation unless the agent has access to the demand *in the sense of consciously believing that it calls for a specific act that he sees himself as able to perform*. However, under this interpretation, the premise is clearly false; for agents are constantly being influenced by normative demands of which they are not conscious at all.

Some of these demands are nonmoral while others are moral. An agent responds unthinkingly to one or more nonmoral demand whenever he reasons in accordance with the rules of logic; whenever he rapidly processes information about the speed, angle, and spin of a baseball that he must hit; and whenever he intuitively arrives at a correct assessment of a complicated body of evidence. An agent responds unthinkingly to a moral demand whenever, as a conscientious person, he automatically does his duty; whenever, as an honest person, he does not even consider lying to extricate himself from a difficult situation; and whenever, as a kindly soul, he unthinkingly steers the conversation away from a hurtful topic. Although these examples differ in important ways, they all converge on the conclusion that many normative demands are constantly influencing each agent's practical deliberation without ever breaking the surface of his consciousness.

Thus, to make true the premise that no normative demand can influence an agent's deliberation unless it is accessible to him, we must interpret accessibility not in terms of conscious awareness, but rather in terms of the demand's ability to make effective contact with the agent's whole cognitive and motivational system—an enormously complex system the vast majority of whose elements are opaque even to the agent himself. However, as so interpreted, our premise is far too weak to support the requisite version of the Kantian Principle. Because it has been tailored to accommodate the fact that agents can be influenced even by normative demands of which they are not aware, the premise as so interpreted does not imply that every demand of which the target agent is unaware must fail to achieve its internal aim. And, for this reason, it also does not imply that any demand of which the target agent is unaware—or, *a fortiori*, the retrospective endorsement of any such demand—is thereby rendered unreasonable.

Up to now, I have operated on the assumption that the internal aim of every demand is simply to elicit the demanded action. As long as the aims of moral and prudential demands are understood in these terms, they will not support the conclusion that it is unreasonable to make—or, therefore, retrospectively to endorse—a demand of which the target agent is not aware. But *should* the internal aims of all demands be understood exclusively in these terms? Isn't there a distinction between demands that address us in our capacity as rational agents and demands that seek to influence us by threat or manipulation? Unlike the demands of drill sergeants or the parents of young children, don't the demands of prudence and morality seek not merely to induce agents to perform the demanded actions, but rather to induce them to do so *for the right reasons*?

The answer, I think, is that this more specific description does capture the internal aims of moral and prudential demands, but that introducing it does not change the argument's basic thrust. Even if each moral demand does seek to induce the target agent to do the right thing for the right reasons, it hardly follows that that aim cannot be achieved unless the agent is conscious of the features of his situation that *provide* him with those reasons. An agent who registers another's distress without bringing it to consciousness, and who unthinkingly adjusts his behavior to defuse the situation, may still be reason-responsive in the full sense.[8] He may still be motivated by either the rational desirability of kindness or a freestanding desire to be kind—take your pick—and it may still be the case that he would not have adjusted his behavior if the other had not given subliminal indications of distress. As this example shows and many others confirm, the mere fact that someone does not consciously register the reason-giving aspects of his situation does not mean that the corresponding moral demand cannot fully achieve its aim. Thus, even if we acknowledge that moral and prudential demands aim not just at eliciting the demanded actions but rather at eliciting their performance for the right reasons, we will still be able to say that retrospectively endorsing a demand of whose factual basis the target agent was not aware—and so, by extension, blaming or holding that agent responsible for not meeting that demand—is not necessarily unreasonable.

Might someone block this conclusion by insisting on a still more stringent characterization of the internal aims of moral and prudential demands? Might someone insist, in particular, that those demands aim not merely at inducing agents to perform the right actions, nor yet at inducing agents to perform the right acts for the right reasons, but rather at inducing agents to perform the right actions for the right reasons *through the recognition of those reasons*. Although his topic is not exactly the internal aims of moral demands, Thomas Scanlon comes close to endorsing a proposal of this sort when he writes that

> real governance, in the sense presupposed by moral interaction, requires not only the right kind of regular connection between action "outputs" and the reason-giving force of the considerations presented as "inputs" but something more, namely, that these "outputs" depend at crucial junctures on the force that these considerations *seem to the agent* to have.[9]

8. For resourceful defense of this claim, see Nomy Arpaly, *Unprincipled Virtue: An Inquiry into Moral Agency* (Oxford: Oxford University Press, 2003), chapter 2 and *passim*.
9. Scanlon, *What We Owe to Each Other*, 282.

Because it does not seem possible to be conscious of the reasons for doing something without also being conscious of whatever features of one's situation provide one with those reasons, this proposal may indeed imply that it is unreasonable to make, and therefore also retrospectively to endorse, any moral or prudential demand of whose factual basis the target agent was unaware.

But why, exactly, should we accept so stringent a view of the internal aims of moral demands? I can think of two reasons, neither of them persuasive. The first, which takes as its point of departure Scanlon's central idea that an act's rightness depends on its conformity to principles that no one could reasonably reject, is that any attempt either to arrive at such a set of principles or to justify one's conduct in terms of them would require a communicative framework within which agents understood and gave conscious thought to what others had said. The second reason, more directly related to Scanlon's actual point in the quoted passage, is that if an entity such as a computer were programmed to respond to moral demands without ever being conscious of them, then although its behavior might indeed be governed by those demands, it would not be *self*-governing in the full sense.

However, while both of these claims seem true, neither seems strong enough to support the proposed account of the aims of moral demands. In both cases, what the proffered claim succeeds in establishing is not that each and every moral demand must seek to influence the target agent's behavior through his recognition of the reason it provides, but at most that no moral demand can hope to achieve its internal aim unless the target agent is conscious *of much else*. This conclusion, though important, is far too weak to support the view that any demand of which the target agent is unaware is *ipso facto* unreasonable. A *fortiori*, it is also too weak to support the conclusion that the retrospective endorsement of any demand of which the target agent is unaware is *ipso facto* unreasonable. Thus, pending some further argument of a kind that I cannot now envision, we may safely reject the attempt to ground a version of the Kantian Principle that supports the searchlight view in the internal aims of moral or prudential demands.

FIVE

KNEW—OR SHOULD HAVE KNOWN?

THE TWO MOST PROMISING ATTEMPTS TO GROUND THE SEARCHLIGHT
view in the demands of the deliberative perspective have now been seen
to fail. To a committed proponent of the searchlight view, this will simply
mean that we must seek that view's justification elsewhere. However, to
anyone who is *not* antecedently committed to the searchlight view, the
paucity of live alternative justifications, together with the wide array of
contexts in which that view fails to capture our intuitive judgments, will
add up to a good (though still provisional) case for understanding the
epistemic condition for responsibility differently. In the current chapter,
I begin the long trek toward a more adequate account.

I

The searchlight view conflicts systematically with our intuitions about
agents such as Alessandra, Julian, and the rest. Although none of these
agents are aware that they are acting wrongly or foolishly, most if not all
of them still seem responsible for doing so. Thus, to improve on the
searchlight view, we will have to interpret the epistemic condition in a
way that explains why they remain responsible.

As we have seen, one familiar explanation of why Alessandra,
Julian, and the others remain responsible is that each of them *should*

be aware that he is acting wrongly or foolishly. Putting the same point differently, many would say that each is responsible because a reasonable person in his situation *would* be aware that his act was wrong or foolish. In chapter 2, I argued that this proposal cannot save the searchlight view because adopting it would mean attributing responsibility to many agents from whom the searchlight view explicitly withholds it. However, although this objection decisively shows that we cannot invoke the current proposal to *defend* the searchlight view, it has no comparable weight against the very different strategy of adopting the proposal *in place of* the searchlight view.

Let us therefore look more closely at the proposal that the epistemic condition for responsibility contains a normative element. In its simplest version, this proposal takes the epistemic condition to be *entirely* normative: it asserts that even when someone is aware that he is acting wrongly or foolishly, what matters is not *that* he is aware of this but simply that he *should* be. However, when the proposal is put this way, it distorts what is significant about cases in which agents knowingly and willingly act wrongly or foolishly. In these cases, what matters is precisely what the agents actually do realize. For this reason, the more promising version of the proposal is disjunctive. As so interpreted, it allows an agent to satisfy the epistemic condition in either of two ways: first, by actually being aware that his act is wrong or foolish, but also, second, by being in a situation in which he should be aware of this. On this disjunctive account, the condition remains recognizably epistemic because each of its disjuncts contains an ineliminable reference to the agent's awareness. However, because the reference in the second disjunct is embedded in a normative context—because it is governed by a deontic operator—that disjunct nevertheless implies that agents can be responsible for features of their act of which they are not aware.

I suspect that many who are attracted to the searchlight view would accept this proposal as a friendly amendment. At any rate, something very like it appears to underlie much that philosophers and legal theorists actually say. It seems, for example, to be implicit in each of the following quotations, the first two of which appear in the philosophical literature while the third is from the American Law Institute's *Model Penal Code*:

Although we can sometimes disclaim responsibility by saying "I did not know" or "I did not realize", we often counter that disclaimer with the retort "Well, you should have known."[1]

In English there is a commonly-used locution to describe the purely negligent agent. We say that although she did not realize at the time that she was violating a norm she *should* have realized it.[2]

A person acts negligently with respect to a material element of an offense when he should be aware of a substantial and unjustifiable risk that the material element exists or will result from his conduct. The risk must be of such a nature and degree that the actor's failure to perceive it, considering the nature and purpose of his conduct, the circumstances known to him and the care that would be exercised by a reasonable person in his situation, involves substantial culpability.[3]

Should we, too, accept a proposal along these lines?

Before we can decide, we will have to answer a number of hard questions, some of which concern the proposal's meaning while others concern its relation to the broader concept of responsibility. The central question about the proposal's meaning concerns the import of its "should." When we say that someone should have been aware that he was acting wrongly or foolishly, what kind of normative assertion are we making? Are we saying only that the agent had evidence that his act *was* wrong or foolish? Does the relevant "should" pertain strictly to the relation between the latter proposition and whichever other propositions or facts constituted the agent's evidence? Or are we saying, instead or in addition, that the agent himself has somehow fallen short? If we are saying this, do we simply mean that the agent has failed to acquire a (conscious) belief for which he had good evidence? Or do we mean instead that the agent has failed to do something that, had he done it, would have caused him *to* acquire that belief? If there is something that the agent has failed to do, does it consist simply of paying close attention to his situation or the beliefs about it that constitute

1. J. R. Lucas, *Responsibility* (Oxford: Oxford University Press, 1993), 52.

2. Steven Sverdlik, "Pure Negligence," *American Philosophical Quarterly* 30 (April 1993), 141.

3. "Model Penal Code," 2.02 (d), in Herbert Morris, ed., *Freedom and Responsibility: Readings in Philosophy and Law* (Stanford, CA: Stanford University Press, 1961), 237.

his evidence? Or does it consist rather of undertaking some more overt course of action—asking questions, for example, or conducting some sort of inquiry—that in its turn would have led him to acquire the relevant belief?

Even by themselves, these questions are difficult. However, they become more difficult yet when we ask why it should *matter* whether an agent has fallen short in any of these ways. To bring out what is troublesome about this question, we need only remind ourselves of the role that an agent's actually being aware that he is acting wrongly or foolishly is standardly thought to play in rendering him responsible for acting that way. Roughly speaking, the reason the agent's actual awareness seems significant is that it implies that the act's being wrong or foolish is among the total set of considerations in light of which he chose to perform it. To whatever extent his choice was in this way knowing as well as willing, the act, qua instance of wrong or foolish behavior, is in a suitably deep sense his own. However, and in stark contrast, when an agent merely *should* be aware that he is acting wrongly or foolishly, there is no comparably direct connection between the wrongness or foolishness of what he does and his informed will. Hence, where no actual awareness is involved, the standard rationale for holding him responsible does not appear to be available.

Before we can ask how the premise that an agent should be aware that he is acting wrongly or foolishly might support the conclusion that he is responsible for doing so, we will have to fix the meaning of the relevant "should." This suggests that we should try to resolve the analytical question before we turn to the more substantive one. Unfortunately, when we survey the literature, we find that no single interpretation of the relevant "should" stands out. Those who use the term in this connection rarely define it, and different thinkers appear to use it differently. Hence, instead of restricting our attention to any single interpretation of the claim that an agent should be aware that he is acting wrongly or foolishly—for brevity, I will from now on refer to this claim as S—we will have to work systematically through its interpretations. As we do, the question to keep in mind is whether *any* interpretation of S might allow us to understand how its truth can render someone responsible for his wrong or foolish act. As we will see, the answer to this question is an emphatic "no."

II

Let us begin with S's weakest interpretation, which takes it to assert only that the agent has good evidence that his act is wrong or foolish. Put a bit more expansively, this weakest interpretation takes the claim that an agent should be aware that he is acting wrongly or foolishly to assert only that

> (S1) there is some sort of deductive or probabilistic or evidential relation between something else that the agent believes, or some aspect of his situation, and the proposition that his act is wrong or foolish.

But can the truth of this version of S really explain why the person of whom it is true is *responsible* for the act of whose wrongness or foolishness he is unaware?

One obvious problem with this proposal is that many of the agents whom we take to be responsible for acts of whose wrongness or foolishness they are unaware are also unaware of anything that might constitute evidence that those acts *are* wrong or foolish. Thus, to revert to two of our previous examples, Alessandra has forgotten all about Sheba and so is not aware that she is suffering in the hot car, while Wren has fallen asleep and so is not aware of anything. A different but closely related problem is that even many agents who *are* aware of facts or propositions that constitute their evidence that they are acting wrongly or foolishly are not aware of the evidential relations that confer this status *upon* those facts or propositions. Thus, even if Scout is in some sense aware both that alcohol is toxic and that babies are delicate, she is evidently *not* aware of the further fact that the combination of these facts makes it wrong for her to give vodka to the baby.

These considerations do not prevent us from saying that Alessandra, Wren, and Scout *have* good evidence that they are acting wrongly, but they do compel us to locate that evidence exclusively in the relations among certain facts or propositions of which, or of whose significance, they are unaware. This makes it hard to see how the truth of S, construed simply as the claim that the agents have such evidence, can render them responsible for acting wrongly. For how can any mere abstract relation among a set of facts or propositions and the further proposition that a given act is wrong or foolish bring the person who performs the act into a close enough relation to its wrongness or foolishness to justify us in blaming, punishing, or making him pay the price for it?

To answer this question without strengthening our interpretation of S, we must somehow establish that the evidential relations among these particular facts or propositions have real implications about the agent's moral status. I can think of two possible ways of doing this. One strategy is to invoke the premise that at least some of the facts or propositions that constitute an agent's evidence that he is acting wrongly or foolishly are bound to be facts or propositions about *him*, while another is to point out that the existence of these facts, or the truth of these propositions, is bound to raise the probability that the agent would be right if he *were* to view his act as wrong or foolish. However, on closer inspection, neither strategy connects the agent to the wrongness or foolishness of his act in the right way.

For suppose, first, that we try to bring the agent back into the picture by arguing that at least some of the facts or propositions that constitute his evidence that he is acting wrongly or foolishly are sure to be facts or propositions about him. About this proposal, the obvious question is why his being involved in the evidence-constituting facts or propositions in this way should matter. If some of the facts or propositions that constituted an agent's evidence that he was acting wrongly or foolishly were facts or propositions about (say) Charles de Gaulle or Lassie or the Grand Canyon, would it follow that de Gaulle or Lassie or the Grand Canyon was responsible for the agent's wrong or foolish act? If not, why should a comparable line of reasoning be any more convincing when the evidence-constituting facts or propositions are facts or propositions about the agent himself?

The other proposed way of bringing the agent back into the picture—to argue that the evidence of his act's wrongness or foolishness raises the likelihood that he would be right if he *were to* regard it as wrong or foolish—is no better. Here again, the question is why this implication of the facts or propositions that constitute the agent's evidence should have anything to do with his being responsible. How can any mere increase in the likelihood that the agent would be right if he were to believe that his act was wrong or foolish render him responsible for performing the act if he doesn't in fact hold this belief? Why should the truth of any such counterfactual have any bearing on whether the agent actually is responsible? Given the categorical nature of our attributions of responsibility, mustn't the facts about agents upon which they depend be categorical as well?

If, as I think, the answer to this last question is "yes," then anyone who takes the truth of S to satisfy the epistemic condition for responsibility will have to move to a stronger interpretation of its "should." Instead of taking S to assert only that some set of propositions that the agent believes, or some set of facts about his situation, renders it likely or certain that he is acting wrongly or foolishly, we will also (or instead) have to take S to say something categorical about the agent's lack of responsiveness *to* those propositions or facts. But what, exactly, could its categorical claim amount to?

III

There are a number of ways in which we might strengthen our interpretation of S, and I will turn shortly to an examination of them. However, before I do, I want to introduce, and explain the rationale for, a change in the terminology that I have been using.

Up to now, I have been referring to the beliefs and aspects of the agent's situation that stand in either evidential or probabilistic or deductive relations to the proposition that his act is wrong or foolish as his *evidence* for that proposition. This way of speaking goes beyond ordinary usage by implying that the evidence for a proposition need not be empirical, but it provides a way of capturing the thought that we are dealing exclusively with an abstract relation involving only facts or propositions (or, at most, the propositional contents of beliefs). However, as soon as we abandon our original weak interpretation of S in favor of something stronger, we will move from the antiseptic world of relations among facts and propositions to the more human world in which persons do or do not hold the beliefs that their evidence supports. To mark this transition, I will no longer refer to the relevant beliefs and aspects of an agent's situation as his evidence that he is acting wrongly or foolishly, but will instead refer to them as his *reasons* for believing this.

Bearing this terminological change in mind, let us ask how we might strengthen our interpretation of S's claim that an agent should have been aware that he was acting wrongly or foolishly. Listing the possibilities in ascending order of strength, we might augment our original interpretation by taking S to assert either that

> (S2) the agent failed to realize that he was acting wrongly or foolishly despite the reasons for believing this with which his other beliefs or the facts of his situation provided him; or

> (S3) the agent fell short of some applicable standard by failing to realize that he was acting wrongly or foolishly despite the reasons for believing this with which his other beliefs or the facts of his situation provided him; or

> (S4) the agent fell short of some applicable standard by failing to do something that would have led him to realize that he was acting wrongly or foolishly on the basis of the reasons with which his other beliefs or the facts of his situation provided him.

To complete our discussion of the prospects for recasting the epistemic condition for responsibility in terms of S, we must now ask whether any of these versions of S will enable us to understand how an agent's satisfying that epistemic condition might bring him into an appropriate relation to the wrongness or foolishness of what he does.

Let us begin with S2, which takes S to assert that the agent failed to recognize his act as wrong or foolish despite the reasons for believing this with which his evidence provided him. Because S2 is a direct implication of the combination of S1's claim that the agent had reason to believe that his act was wrong or foolish and the further fact that he didn't (consciously) hold that belief, there is a sense in which this interpretation doesn't add much to S1. Still, it does add something insofar as it builds the relevant implication right into S's content. Thus, our first question is whether this minimal addition might allow us to invoke S to explain how an agent who acts wrongly or foolishly without being aware of it can nevertheless be responsible for doing so.

At first glance, this strategy for explaining the agent's responsibility may appear to founder on the fact that every proposition that any agent believes, and a fortiori every fact about his situation, is deductively and probabilistically and evidentially related to indefinitely many (other) propositions that he *might* believe. Because the number of propositions that each person has good reason to believe is so much larger than the number of beliefs that anyone can consciously hold, it may seem implausible to suppose that merely failing to respond to one's reasons for believing that a certain act would have a certain feature can render one responsible for performing an act that has that feature. However, to this objection it can be replied that even if most of the implications of what each agent believes are indeed irrelevant to what he is responsible for doing, there are many possible criteria—salience, ease of inference, and relevance to the interests of the agent or others are three—by which the implication that he is acting wrongly or foolishly might be set apart from these. Because that implication stands out in so many ways, it is at least not obvious that the current objection succeeds.

Yet even if it does not, a more decisive difficulty will remain. What we are trying to understand is how an agent can be responsible for performing a wrong or foolish act that he did not recognize *as* wrong or foolish. The explanation we are considering is that what makes such an agent responsible is his failure to recognize the force of his reasons for believing that the act *is* wrong or foolish. But if there is a problem about how an agent can be responsible for acting wrongly or foolishly despite his failure to recognize that his *act* is wrong or foolish, then isn't there just as much of a problem about how an agent can be responsible for acting wrongly or foolishly despite his failure to recognize his *reasons for believing* that his act is wrong or foolish? If we are trying to link the act's wrongness or foolishness to the agent in some suitably strong sense, then how does it help to relocate the point at which the crucial failure of recognition occurs? Even if we replace the claim that the agent has failed to recognize his act's wrongness or foolishness with the claim that what he has failed to recognize are the reasons that his situation or other beliefs gave him for believing that his act *was* wrong or foolish, won't it remain true that the act's wrongness or foolishness played no role in his practical reasoning? And, as long as this is true, won't the question of how the act's wrongness or foolishness can be attributed to him in any sense that is strong enough to justify blaming or punishing him for it remain unanswered?

IV

These considerations suggest that S will not support the claim that a given agent is responsible for an act that he did not recognize as wrong or foolish if all that it categorically asserts about him is that he failed to recognize the force of his reasons for believing that the act *was* wrong or foolish. Because a failure to recognize the force of one's reasons is simply a nonevent, this categorical assertion conveys no positive information about the agent. For this reason, it provides us with no basis upon which to connect his act's wrongness or foolishness to him.

Given this difficulty, the obvious next move is to augment our interpretation of S yet again, this time by taking it to say something further about the agent's failure to respond to his reasons for believing that his act was wrong or foolish. On one influential construal, S's further assertion consists precisely of the claim that the agent's failure to respond to these reasons fell short of some standard of rationality or reasonableness. This addition, which moves us from S2 to S3, is implicit in many versions of the law's contention that whether someone has acted negligently depends on whether a reasonable person in his situation would have recognized the act as one he should not perform.

We have already encountered one statement of this "reasonable person" test. A few pages back, it surfaced in an auxiliary capacity in the quoted passage from the *Model Penal Code*, which backs its definition of a negligent agent as one who should be aware of the risky nature of his conduct with a reference to "the care that would be exercised by a reasonable person." By contrast, in many other places, the reasonable-person test is advanced as freestanding. For example, Herbert Morris has written that where negligence is concerned, "[t]he question asked is, 'Did the man act as a reasonable and prudent man would have acted in his circumstances?' "[4] In either its auxiliary or its freestanding employment, the central function of the claim that a reasonable person would not have acted as the agent did is precisely to call attention to a standard of reasonableness relative to which the agent's action fell short. In the words of H. L. A. Hart, the claim "refer[s] to the fact that the agent failed to comply with a standard of conduct with which any ordinary reasonable man *could* and *would* have complied: a standard requiring him to take precautions against harm."[5]

---

4. Herbert Morris, "Negligence, Recklessness, and Strict Liability," in Morris, ed., *Freedom and Responsibility*, 232.

5. H. L. A. Hart, *Punishment and Responsibility: Essays in the Philosophy of Law* (Oxford: Oxford University Press, 1968), 148.

By taking S to assert that there is a gap between what some relevant standard required and what the agent actually believed or did, we will not only construe S as saying something positive about the agent, but will also explicate its "should" in more robustly normative terms than we would by taking it to designate only a relation between the propositional content of a belief that the agent might have held and certain other beliefs or facts. It may therefore seem that adopting this version of S will finally enable us to understand how agents can be responsible for acts of whose wrongness or foolishness they were unaware. Unfortunately, despite the vigor with which Hart presses this suggestion, it is hard to see how the argument might work.

A preliminary problem with this proposal, which I do not intend to pursue, is that it is unclear whether the standard to whose violation S3 refers is best taken as epistemic or moral/prudential. The epistemic reading is suggested by the fact that the standard is one that governs the formation of beliefs on the basis of evidence, while the moral/prudential reading is suggested by the role that the standard is said to play in determining the agent's responsibility. However, having mentioned this unclarity, I shall for the moment set it aside; for the central objection to the current proposal will apply under either interpretation of the relevant standard.

Perhaps predictably, the central objection is that the proposal is another sideways move. To see this, we must first remind ourselves that anyone who acts wrongly or foolishly is of necessity already violating one moral or prudential standard—namely, the standard with reference to which his act *is* wrong or foolish. Because what we are trying to understand is precisely how such an agent can be responsible for acting wrongly or foolishly despite not being aware of violating this standard, the mere fact that he *is* violating it is evidently not sufficient to establish his responsibility. However, if the agent's unrecognized violation of the original standard is not sufficient to tie him closely enough to his act's wrongness or foolishness to render him responsible for it, then why should his equally unrecognized violation of any further moral or prudential or epistemic standard tie him any *more* closely to it? However many standards someone manages to violate when (say) he forgets an important appointment, Hart's opponents are surely right to insist that "the thought of the engagement never comes into his mind"[6] and that "[t]he man's mind is a blank as

---

6. Glanville Williams, *Textbook of Criminal Law* (London: Stevens & Sons, 1978), 46.

to the consequences in question."[7] Thus, if it is problematic to hold someone responsible for violating a standard of morality or prudence whose applicability to his situation he has failed to recognize, then it will hardly help matters to add that his failure to recognize that standard's applicability also places him in violation of a further standard, this time one which dictates responsiveness to epistemic reasons, whose applicability to his situation he has *also* failed to recognize.

V

Of the three reconstructions of S that we have now examined, each fails for essentially the same reason. Put most simply, the problem in each case is that S as so interpreted does not attribute the wrongness or foolishness of what the agent has done to any significant facts about *him*. This is true whether we take S to assert that the agent had good evidence that his act was wrong or foolish; whether we take it to assert that the agent failed to recognize the force of the reasons that this evidence provided; or whether we take it to assert that the agent's not recognizing the force of those reasons represented a failure to live up to some epistemic, moral, or prudential standard. Because all three versions of S focus either on what the agent did not recognize or do or on what was wrong with his not recognizing or doing it, none sheds any light on the internal workings of the process through which the not-recognizing or the not-doing came about. For this reason, none provides us with the resources that we need to connect the act's wrongness or foolishness to the agent himself.

All this may appear to change, however, when we switch over to the remaining possible interpretation of S. According to this last interpretation, S4, what we mean when we say that an agent should have been aware that he was acting wrongly or foolishly is that he has fallen short by not doing something that, had he done it, would have led him to recognize his act *as* wrong or foolish. If we can hold the agent primarily responsible for some earlier lapse, such as a failure to pay attention or to investigate further, then we can hold him derivatively responsible for his

---

7. J. W. C. Turner, *The Modern Approach to Criminal Law* (London: MacMillan and Co., 1945), 211; quoted in Hart, *Punishment and Responsibility*, 148–49.

subsequent lack of awareness of the act's wrongness or foolishness. Given this proposal's obvious appeal, it is not surprising that we find echoes of it even in Hart's defense of the ostensibly quite different view that what renders the negligent agent responsible is simply his act's failure to come up to some appropriate standard. There is, for example, more than a hint of the idea that that failure can be traced to some earlier omission in Hart's characterization of it as a "failure to exercise the capacity to advert to, and to think about and control, conduct and its risks."[8]

But, given what has been said, I think it is clear that this proposal is no more promising than its predecessors. The difficulty can be put as a dilemma. Suppose first that S4 asserts only that the agent failed to pay sufficient attention or investigate sufficiently, but not that he consciously chose to refrain from doing these things. In that case, many if not all of the agents in our original nine examples will indeed satisfy S4, but our original question—how can someone be responsible for an omission of which he was unaware—will merely reappear as a question about their failure to pay attention or investigate. This, clearly, will gain us no ground. Suppose, next, that S4 asserts not merely that the agent failed to pay sufficient attention or investigate sufficiently, but also that he consciously chose not to do these things. If we adopt this reading, and take S4 to assert that the agent has knowingly and willingly assumed the risk of subsequently doing something wrong, then it will indeed be clear how someone who satisfies S4 can be responsible for his subsequent unwitting wrong act, but it will also be true that most of the unwitting wrongdoers who seem responsible for what they have done, including all nine agents in our original examples, will not be *among* those who satisfy S4. As we saw, there was no earlier point at which Alessandra decided not to think about the danger to Sheba, at which Julian decided to ignore the looming rocks, or at which any of our other agents consciously turned his attention away from the wrong-making features of what he would subsequently do. Hence, on this reading, too, S4 will fail to explain what needs to be explained.

There is one further possibility that warrants brief mention, and that is the possibility of avoiding the dilemma by going between its horns. To avoid the difficulty in this way, we would have to read S4 as attributing the agent's failure to pay attention or investigate to something less than a fully conscious choice, but to something more than

8. Hart, "Negligence, Mens Rea, and Criminal Responsibility," 157.

a simple lack of awareness that there is anything to attend to or investigate. We would, in other words, have to take S4's version of the epistemic condition to assert that when an agent has fallen short of some applicable standard by failing to do something that would have led him to recognize that his projected act was wrong or foolish, he is not responsible for that act unless he was at least inchoately aware that there might be something wrong with what he was about to do.

But far from taking us between the horns of the dilemma, this maneuver will succeed only at impaling us on both of them. The second horn, which asserts that most of the unwitting wrongdoers who seem responsible have not consciously chosen to refrain from paying attention or investigating, will still get us because many such wrong-doers have also not chosen to ignore any ambiguous warning signs. This is the most natural reading of *Hot Dog*, in which Alessandra's attention was instantaneously captured by the imbroglio at the school, of *Home for the Holidays*, in which Joliet's surge of panic made reasoned choice impossible, and, I think, of the majority of our other cases. Moreover, even in the minority of cases in which the agent can be viewed as having had some inkling that he was running a moral risk, that fact does not blunt the dilemma's first horn enough to prevent it from puncturing the case for adopting S4.

To see why this is so, let us now stipulate that some of our agents *were* inchoately aware that they were not guarding against error with sufficient care. Let us suppose, for example, that Julian's fantasy became progressively less satisfying as his ferry approached the rocks, that Ryland noticed a darkening of the emotional skies as she prepared to deliver her punch line, and that Scout felt a flicker of doubt as she decanted the vodka into the fruit juice. Even under these new assumptions, there remains a significant cognitive gap between what each agent chose—namely, not to follow up on an ambiguous and visceral warning sign—and the wrongness of the act that followed. A small still voice is, after all, still and small. Because an intimation of danger is by its nature indistinct, such an intimation is just too indefinite to sustain the conclusion that choosing not to follow up on it is tantamount to choosing to perform the wrong or foolish act whose true nature a further investigation would have disclosed. Thus, although an unwitting wrongdoer's decision to ignore the warning signs may indeed compound the wrongness of what he has done, it can hardly provide the needed explanation of why he is responsible for doing it.

SIX

A NEW BEGINNING

OUR FIRST ANSWER TO THE QUESTION OF HOW AGENTS CAN BE responsible for acts of whose wrongness or foolishness they are un-aware—that they are responsible when and because they *should* be aware that they are acting wrongly or foolishly—was not a resounding success. Nevertheless, despite that answer's inadequacy, there remains a striking correlation between our willingness to say that an agent should have been aware that he was acting wrongly or foolishly and our willingness to hold him responsible for doing so. Given this correlation, it is hard to believe that there is *no* connection between what an agent should have been aware of and what he is responsible for. Thus, the natural next question is whether we might reconstruct whatever connection there is in some less direct way.

I

To get a sense of the possibilities, let us remind ourselves of what was wrong with the direct approach. In the previous chapter, I argued that when an agent should, but does not, recognize that he is acting wrongly or foolishly—when he fails to respond to the beliefs or aspects of his situation that constitute his evidence—this failure cannot by itself ren-der him responsible because it is a mere nonevent that involves no positive facts about him. This remains true even if the resulting lack of awareness causes him to fall below some applicable standard. However, it is one thing to say that an agent's failure to respond to his evidence involves no positive facts about him, and quite another to say that what *accounts for* that failure *also* involves no positive facts about him. In many (though not all) cases, the facts that explain why an agent fails to realize that he is acting wrongly or foolishly are indeed facts about his own psychology, broadly construed. Taking my cue from this, I now want to consider the possibility that it is precisely these causally effective psychological facts that make it possible to understand how agents can be responsible for acts of whose wrongness or foolishness they are unaware.

Let me begin by sketching, in very broad strokes, the view that I will explore. When I speak of the psychological facts that determine what agents do and do not recognize, I have in mind the full range of attitudes, traits, and dispositions whose interaction determines this. These attitudes, traits, and dispositions include, among many other things, the preoccupations that determine what an agent does and does not notice in different situations, the beliefs that determine what he takes to be evidence for what, the patterns of association that determine what does and does not come into his mind when he is prompted in various ways, and the underlying mechanisms, both physical and nonphysical, that shape his emotional reactions and the speed and accuracy of his inferences and decision-making. Far more than any specifics about what goes on in a person's consciousness, these are the patterns of which we become aware when we spend time with him. To come to know someone's characteristic tendencies of thought is, quite precisely, to come to know *him*.

And, because it is, the psychological features that account for an agent's failure to respond to his evidence that he is acting wrongly or foolishly are often positive facts about him in a strong sense. They have that status whenever they play a significant enough role in making him the person he is. Following up on this, I now want to consider the possibility that when someone is responsible for an act whose wrongness or foolishness he should but does not recognize, the facts that connect him to the act's wrongness or foolishness in a way that justifies us in holding him responsible are precisely those aspects of his mental makeup—whatever they are—that prevent him from gaining access to, or from effectively processing, the information that constitutes his evidence that the act *is* wrong or foolish. Putting the same point a bit differently, I want to consider the possibility that when an agent should, but does not, recognize that he is acting wrongly or foolishly, what connects him to the act's wrongness or foolishness in a way that allows us to hold him responsible is not just his failure to live up to whatever standard requires that those in his position recognize such acts as wrong or foolish, but is rather the whole collection of attitudes, dispositions, and traits whose interaction *causes* him not to recognize this.

In the previous chapter, I suggested that the most promising way of moving beyond the searchlight view is to interpret the epistemic condition for responsibility as a disjunction of which the searchlight view is the first disjunct. As a first attempt to do this, I took the epistemic condition to assert that an agent is not responsible for his wrong or foolish act unless he *either is or should be* aware that he is acting wrongly or foolishly. Because the current proposal builds on this idea, it is best read as preserving the previous interpretation's disjunctive structure while adding an element to its second disjunct. As so elaborated, its second disjunct will assert that someone who is unaware that he is acting wrongly or foolishly is only responsible for doing so if his failure to recognize his act as wrong or foolish is both defective in relation to some applicable standard ("he should have realized") and due to some combination of his own constitutive attitudes, dispositions, and traits.

But why, having come this far, should we retain the reference to what the agent should have realized? Why take the second disjunct of the epistemic condition to require both that the agent's failure to recognize his act as wrong or foolish be due to the interaction of his constitutive attitudes, dispositions, and traits *and* that his state of awareness fell short of some applicable standard? Instead, why not eliminate the reference to what the agent should have realized, and say that when someone does not realize that he is acting wrongly or foolishly, what renders him responsible is just that his failure to recognize his act as wrong or foolish *is* traceable to the interaction of his constitutive attitudes, dispositions, and traits?

Put most simply, the reason we must preserve the reference to what the agent should have realized is that without it the epistemic condition is far too easy to satisfy. Because the scope of an agent's awareness is *always* determined by his psychological makeup—because each of us would realize much more if our observational and inferential abilities were more acute and much less if they were less acute—the proposed simplification would implausibly expand the number of unwitting wrongdoers and foolish agents who would count as responsible. For example, it might compel us to count as responsible the victim of a sudden heart attack (since someone more attuned to his body would have realized that something was amiss and sought medical attention), the teacher whose chance remark precipitates a suicide (since someone with greater psychological insight would have recognized the warning signs), and perhaps even the pedestrian who is swallowed by a sinkhole (since someone with X-ray eyes would have seen the earth opening). What separates these agents from, for example, the Scout of *Colicky Baby* is not that their failures to realize that they are acting wrongly or foolishly cannot be traced to their constitutive attitudes, dispositions, and traits, but rather that the states of awareness to which those attitudes, traits, and dispositions give rise are in no way defective. Thus, to preserve the conclusion that such agents are not responsible, we must indeed insist that those who unwittingly perform wrong or foolish acts are only responsible if their states of awareness are defective.

With this requirement included, the partial version of the epistemic condition that I am proposing is

> PEC: When someone performs a wrong or foolish act in a way that satisfies the voluntariness condition, and when he also satisfies any other conditions for responsibility that are independent of the epistemic condition, he is responsible for his act's wrongness or foolishness if, but only if, he either
>
> (1) is aware that the act is wrong or foolish when he performs it, or else
>
> (2) is unaware that the act is wrong or foolish despite having evidence for its wrongness or foolishness his failure to recognize which
> (a) falls below some applicable standard, and
> (b) is caused by the interaction of some combination of his constitutive attitudes, dispositions, and traits.

Because PEC does not purport to specify the conditions under which agents are responsible for acts that are *not* wrong or foolish—because it says nothing about responsibility for acts that are morally neutral or obligatory or supererogatory or that benefit or at least do not harm the agent—it is not a full statement of the epistemic condition. However, as I remarked earlier, it is responsibility for wrongdoing and imprudence that seems both most important and most problematic. Thus, if PEC can at least do justice to the cases in which agents seem responsible for acts that are wrong or foolish, we may reasonably hope to deal with the remaining cases later.

II

But *does* PEC do justice to the cases in which agents seem responsible for acts that are wrong or foolish? To answer this question, we will have to ascertain, first, whether (just about) every agent who intuitively seems responsible for a wrong or foolish act has satisfied either (1) or (2), and, second, whether these agents' having satisfied (1) or (2) is part of an adequate explanation of *why* they are responsible for what they did. In the chapters that follow, I will argue for a positive answer to the second question. However, before I can get to that, I must establish that the class of agents who satisfy either (1) or (2) (and who also satisfy any non-epistemic requirements for responsibility) is roughly coextensive with the class of agents who seem responsible for their wrong or foolish acts.

There is little doubt that someone who satisfies (1)'s requirement that he realize that he is acting wrongly or foolishly, and who also satisfies all the non-epistemic requirements, is responsible for what he does. It is precisely the clarity of such cases that has led many to accept the searchlight view. But what of those who seem responsible for acting wrongly or foolishly *without* being aware of it? What of the agents who were introduced as counterexamples to the searchlight view? Do Alessandra, Julian, and the others really satisfy both (2a), the requirement that their responses to their evidence that they are acting wrongly or foolishly fall below the applicable standards, and (2b), the requirement that their failures to recognize their acts as wrong or foolish be traceable to their constitutive traits, attitudes, and dispositions?

To answer this question fully, I would have to provide a much more detailed account of (2)'s key terms than I have yet done. I would, in particular, have to spell out both the standards that determine what an agent in a given situation should be aware of and the criteria that determine when a given trait, attitude, or disposition is constitutive of its possessor. However, although both topics clearly require, and will receive, careful attention, we can reach a preliminary answer without addressing them. Even in their current rough form, requirements (2a) and (2b) are pretty clearly satisfied by most if not all of our original nine agents.

There is, I think, little doubt that all nine agents satisfy (2a). It was, after all, precisely our sense that Alessandra, Julian, and the others should have realized that they were acting wrongly or foolishly, and that the gap between what they should have realized and what they did realize makes some important contribution to their responsibility, that initially tempted us to interpret the relevant disjunct of the epistemic condition exclusively in these terms. Hence, as long as we take each agent's situation to encompass only facts external to him rather than "internal" facts such as beliefs and psychological traits—an interpretation I will defend in due course—we may safely assume that all nine agents have failed to meet whatever standards determine what agents in their situations should be aware of.

The more interesting question is whether most if not all of them also satisfy (2b). When Alessandra, Julian, and the others fail to meet the standards that determine what agents in their situations should be aware of, can their epistemic shortcomings be traced to the psychological features that make them the individuals they are? Can we plausibly say of each agent that his failure to recognize his act's wrongness or foolishness is caused by some combination of his constitutive traits, attitudes, and dispositions?

To get clearer about this, let us begin with the cases I dubbed *Colicky Baby*, *Bad Joke*, *Bad Policy*, and *Bad Weather*. What makes it natural to begin with these cases is that each involves an agent whose character is in some respect worse than normal. This was made explicit in my initial description of Ryland, who was said to be unusually self-absorbed, and of Sylvain, who was said regularly to treat students unequally, and it is a reasonable inference from the behavior of Scout and amerika. Because all four agents can be assumed to have defective characters, the way they satisfy (2b) is especially clear. For example, when Scout fails to realize that she should not give the vodka to the baby, we naturally attribute her failure not to any lack of information—it is, after all, common knowledge that alcohol is toxic and babies delicate—but rather to certain flawed patterns of thought. It is, we assume, some combination of Scout's irresponsibility-related disposi-tions—her impulsiveness, perhaps, or her tendency not to consider the consequences of what she does—that prevents the idea that she may be harming the baby from even entering her mind. And, analogously, when Ryland fails to realize that she should not make jokes about handicaps to people who have them, we naturally attribute this failure not to any lack of knowledge, but rather to whatever combination of traits and attitudes sustains or constitutes the self-absorption that renders her oblivious to other people's feelings. Mutatis mutandis, we make similar assumptions about Sylvain and amerika. In each case, we gravitate naturally to the view that the agent himself—the whole person—is the source of his own failure to appreciate the connection between the facts with which he is acquainted and the wrongness of his act.

Although the fact that these agents have flawed characters makes it especially easy to see how they satisfy (2b), it is important to realize that (2b) can also be satisfied by agents whose characters are *not* flawed. Elsewhere, I have argued that when agents act wrongly, the wrongness of their acts can sometimes be traced to the interaction of many fine-grained dispositions none of which are moral flaws.[1] By a natural extension of this argument, the interaction of many fine-grained dis-positions none of which are moral flaws can also prevent agents from responding to their *evidence* that they are acting wrongly. And, because of this, the same reasoning that shows that the flawed Scout, Ryland, Sylvain, and amerika have probably satisfied (2b) will also show this about at least some of our agents whose characters are not flawed.

To see how the reasoning works in these cases, consider first Alessandra, who is not an irresponsible person, but who does neglect her obligation to protect Sheba on a particular occasion. When Alessandra is wrangling with the teachers at her children's school, she knows that Sheba is in the hot car in precisely the sense in which Ryland knows that jokes about disabilities can be hurtful and Scout knows that babies are physiologically different from adults: although the propos-ition is not before her mind, she would sincerely assent to it if prompted. Moreover, also as in the cases of Ryland and Scout, we

---

1. For defense of this claim, and some illustrations, see chapters 2 and 3 of my book *In Praise of Blame* (Oxford: Oxford University Press, 2006).

naturally assume that Alessandra's failure to react to what she knows by concluding that she should let Sheba out of the car is explained by some further combination of her attitudes and traits. Even if none of these traits or attitudes are bad, it remains true that if they were different enough—if, for example, Alessandra were less solicitous of her children, or was made less anxious by conflict—then she would not have forgotten about the dog. Thus, in *Hot Dog*, no less than in the bad-character cases, we can make sense of the agent's responsibility by taking Alessandra herself—the whole person—to be the source of her own failure to draw the connection between what she knows and the wrongness of her act. And, along similar lines, we can make sense of the idea that Julian is responsible in *On the Rocks* by attributing the erotic fantasy that distracts him from his obligation to steer the ferry to some combination of the traits, attitudes, and dispositions that together make him the person that *he* is.

Our final three cases, *Home for the Holidays*, *Caught off Guard*, and *Jackknife*, are less straightforward; for to bring the proposed explanation to bear on them, we will have to say that the tendency to panic that prevents Joliet from recognizing that she should not pull the trigger is itself part of what makes her the person she is; that Wren would not have fallen asleep if she had cared (even) more about doing her duty; and that the inaccuracy with which Father Poteet processes the visual cues with which he is flooded is itself a reflection of the complex psychology that makes him the person he is. These claims raise questions that their predecessors do not. Are the boundaries of the self really capacious enough to encompass Joliet's tendency to panic? Is Wren best viewed as someone who would have stayed awake if she had cared enough about doing so, or should we instead view her as someone whose brain has mimicked the effects of a sleeping pill that would have excused her if administered secretly by another? Can anything as mechanical as the speed or accuracy with which someone processes visual cues really have anything to do with that person's identity?

Although I am quite comfortable with the suggestion that each of the cited mechanisms is constitutive of its possessor, my proposal would not be affected much if one or more were not. The reason the proposal would not be much affected is not just that it would still capture our intuitions about the majority of our counterexamples to the searchlight view, but is also that the remaining counterexamples are precisely the ones about which our intuitions seem weakest. Although most people would indeed agree that Joliet, Wren, and Father Poteet are responsible, many would do so with considerable hesitation. On the account I am proposing, this hesitation is naturally attributed to our uncertainty about the boundaries of the self. Because we are not sure on which side of that boundary to locate the traits that explain why Joliet, Wren, and Father Poteet have not recognized their acts or omissions as wrong, the account correctly predicts that we will lack confidence in our judgments that they are responsible *for* their wrongful acts or omissions. Thus, whatever we ultimately decide about these cases, the uncertainties that they raise will pose little difficulty for our account.

III

But harder problems lie ahead; for if we adopt the proposed approach, and allow the epistemic condition to be satisfied not only by agents who are aware that their acts are wrong or foolish but also by agents whose failure to realize this is both substandard and explained by certain aspects of their constitutive psychology, then we will have to adjust our thinking about responsibility in a number of other areas. To bring out the degree to which this proposal is destabilizing, I need only make explicit a few of its implications.

An initial problem, briefly mentioned in chapter 1, concerns our ability to explain how agents can be responsible for acts that are right and prudent as well as wrong and foolish. As long as we accept the searchlight view, and insist that agents are responsible only for those features of their acts of which they were antecedently aware, the task of extending our account will pose few problems; for the searchlight view is at least as plausible when applied to positive cases as it is when applied to negative ones. However, if we go beyond the searchlight view, and add that agents can also be responsible for their unwitting wrong or foolish acts as long as their failure to recognize those acts as wrong or foolish is both substandard and explained by their constitutive psychology, then our account will not generalize to the positive cases. When an agent does something *right or prudent* without being aware of it—when, for example, someone inadvertently keeps a promise that he has forgotten making—the fact that his cognitive failure is both substandard and due to his constitutive psychology will hardly imply that he deserves credit as our earlier agents deserved blame. Given this disanalogy, accepting the proposed account will evidently mean having to rethink the relation between our attributions of responsibility for good and bad acts.

It will also mean having to rethink the relation between responsibility's epistemic and voluntariness conditions. As long as we take the epistemic condition to restrict an agent's responsibility to those features of his acts of which he is antecedently aware, we can think of the conscious states that satisfy that condition as working in tandem with the choices that satisfy the voluntariness condition. By illuminating what lies along the various paths down which an agent might go, the searchlight of his consciousness can be imagined as guiding the engine of his will. But if the epistemic condition can also be satisfied by someone who does *not* realize that he is acting wrongly or foolishly, then the relation between what satisfies the two conditions will be much less straightforward. When an agent's psychology prevents him from recognizing a possible act as wrong or foolish, its effect is not to illuminate, but rather to obscure, the nature of the options among which he must choose. Thus, if we accept the common assumption that voluntariness requires conscious choice, then some of the epistemic states that satisfy the current version of the epistemic condition will actually preclude the concurrent satisfaction of the voluntariness condition.

Whether the voluntariness condition can be reconceived in a way that avoids this difficulty is at this point unclear. However, even if it can, there will remain a broader question about whether my proposal is consistent with the common belief that responsibility presupposes *control*. At least offhand, the answer again appears to be "no," since when an agent unwittingly acts wrongly or foolishly, his doing so does not appear to be within his (current) control. Even if his failure to recognize the act as wrong or foolish is due exclusively to the interaction of his constitutive psychological states, the fact that he neither chooses nor even recognizes the events in the causal process seems sufficient to guarantee that he is in control neither of that process nor (therefore) of its outcome. And, for this reason, accepting the current proposal may compel us to reject the common view that agents are responsible only for what is within their control.

Because my proposal has so many troublesome implications, the magnitude of the changes that accepting it would require may seem to tell heavily against it. However, given the manifest inadequacy of the searchlight view (and given the less manifest, but no less real, inadequacy of the attempt to augment that view exclusively with a reference to what the agent should have been aware of), it seems to me that the only direction in which we can go is forward. Because we clearly must abandon the idea that agents are responsible only for what they are conscious of doing, it will of course be necessary to rethink the many further assumptions that presuppose that idea. Thus, the real question is not whether those assumptions must be excised from our account of responsibility, but only whether the concept of responsibility can survive the surgery. If the answer is negative, then that concept is, and always has been, incoherent. However, in the remainder of the book, I will argue that the prognosis is not this grim.

SEVEN

SETTING THE NORMS OF RECOGNITION

ACCORDING TO THE PARTIAL ACCOUNT OF RESPONSIBILITY'S EPISTEMIC condition that I have called PEC, an agent who unwittingly acts wrongly or foolishly (and who satisfies all the other conditions for responsibility) is responsible for doing so if, but only if, he has evidence for the act's wrongness or foolishness his failure to recognize which (a) falls below some applicable standard and (b) is caused by the interaction of some combination of his constitutive mental states. To defend PEC, I will have to say more about both the standards that determine what agents should recognize and the criteria that determine which states are constitutive of their possessors. In this chapter, I begin with the norms of recognition.

I

Intuitively, the distinction between what a person should be aware of and what he cannot be expected to recognize is often clear. We can all agree that the Scout of *Colicky Baby* falls on one side of the line and that the person who is about to be hit by a meteorite falls on the other. However, when we try to reconstruct the content and rationale of the norms that underlie these judgments, we quickly encounter difficulties.

Broadly speaking, there are two main problems, the first of which is that we cannot identify the standards that determine what a person in a given agent's situation should be aware of, or what a reasonable person in his situation would be aware of, without first being able to distinguish facts about the agent *from* facts about his situation. The need to make this distinction is problematic because many significant facts—for example, those that concern an agent's level of intelligence, his prior history, and his moral and nonmoral background beliefs—lie disconcertingly close to the boundary. Thus, it is not immediately clear whether we should say, of, for example, a homeopath who endangers his sick child's life by refusing to authorize a proven therapy, that his failure to recognize his act as wrong is substandard for someone who has easy access to orthodox medical care and the Internet, or that that failure meets the standards that apply to those who have easy access to orthodox medical care and the Internet but who also believe strongly in homeopathy.

The second problem, which cuts across the first, concerns not the division between an agent and his situation, but rather the nature of the standards that apply to agents *in* that situation. Put most simply, the central question here is whether those standards are genuinely normative or merely statistical. When we say that someone should be aware that he is acting wrongly or foolishly, or that a reasonable person in his situation would be aware of this, are we saying only that a typical or average person who found himself in the agent's situation would realize that the act was wrong or foolish, or are we saying rather that the agent has failed to meet a demand whose force is independent of what anyone else in his situation would or would not realize? Is the relevant standard merely a summary of what people in such situations generally recognize, or does it express a freestanding normative requirement? If it does express a genuine normative requirement, is that requirement epistemic, or is it moral or prudential?

Although the relevance of these problems may not be immediately obvious, each is of the first importance for my project. The significance of the first problem is that if the beliefs, desires, and traits that prevent an agent from realizing that he is acting wrongly or foolishly are themselves part *of* his situation, then his resulting lack of awareness cannot fall below the standards that apply to agents *in* his situation. Because the agent's failure to realize that he is acting wrongly or foolishly will not be substandard, PEC's requirement (2a) will not be met, and so PEC will imply that the agent is not responsible for his wrong or foolish act. Thus, if we count such "subjective" facts about the agent as part of his situation, then PEC will at best fail to capture many of our intuitions about which unwitting wrongdoers and foolish agents are responsible and will at worst imply that unwitting wrongdoers and foolish agents never *are* responsible.

PEC will also clash with certain intuitions if the standards to which (2a) refers are merely statistical; for in that case, whether someone's reaction to his evidence that he is acting wrongly or foolishly falls below those standards will depend not only on his reaction's intrinsic features, but also on how it stacks up against the reactions of other people. By thus relativizing each agent's responsibility to how well other agents process *their* evidence, PEC will imply that responsibility is a comparative concept. However, in fact, responsibility is not comparative. If anything about the concept is clear, it is that what any given agent is responsible for is a function only of what he himself has done or failed to do.[1]

Taken together, these considerations define the shape of an adequate interpretation of PEC's condition (2a). To play the role that I have assigned it, that condition must presuppose both a nonsubjective account of the unwitting wrongdoer's situation and a nonstatistical account of the standards that govern what someone in that situation ought to be aware of. Thus, the obvious next question is whether a version of (2a) that embodies both presuppositions can in fact be defended.

---

1. It is important to distinguish between the claim that the standards that determine how well an agent has processed his evidence that he is acting wrongly or foolishly are set by the way others process their evidence, and the very different claim that an agent's evidence that he is acting wrongly or foolishly is *itself* provided by the attitudes of his parents, his teachers, or the other members of his society. Because I am denying only the former claim, my account is consistent with the view that people brought up in slave or caste societies are partially or wholly excused because they do not have reason to regard the relevant forms of behavior as wrong. For relevant discussion, see Michele M. Moody-Adams, "Culture, Responsibility, and Affected Ignorance," *Ethics* 104 (January 1994), 291–309; Gideon Rosen, "Culpability and Ignorance," *Proceedings of the Aristotelian Society* 103 (September 2002), 61–84; and Neil Levy, "Cultural Membership and Moral Responsibility," *The Monist* 86 (2003), 145–63.

II

At first glance, the obvious place to seek an answer appears to be the legal literature; for the reasonable-person standard figures prominently in many areas of the law. That standard is used to determine who is criminally or civilly negligent, who has legitimately acted in self-defense, and who is legally liable in many other contexts. Taking our cue from this, let us begin by asking what light this literature can shed on which version of the reasonable-person standard we should incorporate into our account of moral and prudential responsibility.

The question of which facts about an agent the law should classify as belonging to his situation has occasioned considerable debate. According to Joshua Dressler,

> [t]he traditional rule . . . is that although a defendant's unusual physical characteristics (e.g., blindness), if relevant to the case, are incorporated into the "reasonable person" standard, a defendant's unusual mental characteristics are not.[2]

However, Dressler adds that this rule "is under considerable attack and undergoing significant change,"[3] and that

> there are constant pressures on courts to "subjectivize" the "reasonable person," that is, to incorporate into the "reasonable person" some of the mental and/or physical characteristics of the defendant, or by incorporating in him the defendant's personal life experiences.[4]

Because the legal literature on this topic is both rich and divided, we may reasonably expect it to yield important arguments on both sides of our question.

But, interestingly, it does not. When we look at what legal theorists have actually said in defense of an objective reading of the reasonable-person standard, we find that their arguments do not carry over to the moral or prudential context. Moreover, although the arguments for a

---

2. Joshua Dressler, *Understanding Criminal Law*, 3rd edition (New York: Lexis Publishing, 2001), 132.

3. Dressler, *Understanding Criminal Law*, 132.

4. Dressler, *Understanding Criminal Law*, 132.

subjective reading are of course very different, they, too, do not carry over in any obvious way.

Where the arguments for an objective reading are concerned, the basic problem is that most of them are less concerned with guilt or fault than they are with the efficient administration of the law or the effective control of future behavior. According to most legal theorists, the point of excluding subjective considerations is not to achieve a proper matching of culpability to punishment or of fault to burden-bearing, but is instead to sidestep the difficult task of ascertaining what each particular agent believed or how strong his will was,[5] to avoid having to excuse too many defendants,[6] or to provide each agent with an incentive to know and act on the legally relevant facts.[7] Because these last aims are all practical and forward-looking, they are unlikely to shed much light on the conditions under which agents are morally or prudentially responsible for what they have already done.

Given this difference in orientation, we clearly cannot mine the legal literature to justify the objective reading of the reasonable-person standard that PEC's condition (2a) has been seen to require. But neither, conversely, does anything in that literature show that we *cannot* accept such an objective reading. To see this, and thus to complete our brief excursion into the law, we must now consider the arguments that have put pressure on the courts to subjectivize the reasonable-person standard.

Although our own topic is most closely associated with the legal category of negligence, the most serious of the pressures toward subjectivism arise not in that context, but rather in response to questions about when a reasonable person would, for example, feel offended by sexually suggestive conduct, consent to sexual relations, or kill her

---

5. See, for example, Oliver Wendell Holmes, *The Common Law* (Cambridge, MA: Harvard University Press, 1963), lecture III, and Glanville Williams, *Textbook of Criminal Law* (London: Stevens and Sons, 1978), 49.

6. See Williams, 49.

7. See, for example, Roscoe Pound, *An Introduction to the Philosophy of Law* (New Haven: Yale University Press, 1954), 89–91, and Warren A. Seavey, "Negligence—Subjective or Objective?" in Herbert Morris, ed., *Freedom and Responsibility: Readings in the Philosophy of Law* (Stanford, CA: Stanford University Press, 1961), 255.

abusive husband.[8] Because the main challenge to the objective approach comes from this direction, the natural place to look for its rationale is in the feminist legal literature. Of those feminists who favor subjectivizing the law's version of the reasonable-person standard, some do so on the basis of broad doctrinal commitments—for example, the view that the law's notion of objectivity is inherently male[9]—that cannot be considered here. However, others take that position on what are for us the more interesting grounds that the objective standard is bound to be unfair to those whose visions of reality do not reflect the mainstream view. If any feminist argument is to make contact with our own concerns, it will almost certainly be this one.

The reasoning behind the charge of unfairness is laid out clearly by Dolores Donovan and Stephanie Wildman.[10] Their central premises are, first, that in the law of homicide (and, by extension, in many other areas of the law), legal liability requires mens rea, or a guilty mind; second, that it is impossible to assess an agent's degree of moral culpability (or, by extension, his moral responsibility) without taking account of how his situation appeared to him; and, third, that because the objective version of the reasonable-person standard takes the reasonable person to share the values, outlook, and life experiences of those in the social mainstream, it cannot capture either the social reality or (therefore) the degree of culpability or responsibility of those outside the mainstream. From these premises, Donovan and Wildman conclude that under an objective version of the reasonable-person standard,

> [i]njustice will be perpetrated on those individuals who are understandably provoked to a heat of passion or who understandably believe their lives are endangered under circumstances which would not have provoked or frightened the reasonable man.[11]

8. For a useful overview, see Mayo Moran, *Rethinking the Reasonable Person: An Egalitarian Reconstruction of the Objective Standard* (Oxford: Oxford University Press, 2003).

9. For an influential statement of this view, see Catherine MacKinnon, *Toward a Feminist Theory of the State* (Cambridge, MA: Harvard University Press, 1989). For further references, see the footnotes in Moran, *Rethinking the Reasonable Person*, 199–201.

10. D. A. Donovan and S. M. Wildman, "Is the Reasonable Man Obsolete? A Critical Perspective on Self-Defense and Provocation," *Loyola of Los Angeles Law Review* 14 (1981), 435–68.

11. Donovan and Wildman, 462.

Although Donovan and Wildman think we should altogether dispense with the reasonable-person test, and should replace it with the question of whether the agent himself could fairly have been expected to act differently, they acknowledge that another possible response is to stick with the reasonable person but to take him to have precisely the characteristics of the agent whose legal liability is in question.[12]

As many critics have noted, this argument has implications that many feminists would not welcome; for although a subjectivized reasonable-person standard will indeed support such conclusions as that a reasonable woman would find the crude jokes of her male coworkers offensive, or would find it dangerous to resist the sexual advances of an aggressive and physically imposing man, it will also support such conclusions as that a reasonable man would view the crude jokes as harmless and the woman's lack of resistance as tantamount to consent.[13] However, for present purposes, these considerations are doubly irrelevant. They are irrelevant, first, because the question of whether the Donovan–Wildman argument is feminist-friendly is distinct from the question of whether it is sound, and, second, because both questions differ from our own question of whether that argument can be adapted to yield a subjective account of the reasonable-person test that is applicable in contexts of moral responsibility. Moreover, whatever we say about the argument's feminist-friendliness or soundness, the answer to this last question is a clear "no."

Put most simply, the reason the Donovan–Wildman argument cannot be adapted in this way is that it already *presupposes* a subjective interpretation of the reasonable-person standard as it pertains to moral responsibility. When Donovan and Wildman assert that many homicide defendants who lie outside the social mainstream are not morally culpable because their actions are either "understandable" in light of, or rendered "morally involuntary" by, their personal histories and the beliefs they have formed as a result of those histories, they are clearly

12. In a footnote, Donovan and Wildman say that they reject this move because "retaining the reasonableness standard still places the emphasis on a legal abstraction to the detriment of the accused's social reality" (437, n. 10).

13. See, for example, Donald C. Hubin and Karen Haely, "Rape and the Reasonable Man," *Law and Philosophy* 18 (1999), 113–39, and Moran, *Rethinking the Reasonable Person*, ch. 6.

assuming that when it comes to moral as opposed to legal responsibility, what matter are not the actual facts about what an agent did, but rather the facts as he saw them. They are therefore also assuming that if any version of the reasonable-person test is to apply in the context of moral responsibility, it will have to be one that asserts that an agent is only morally responsible if a reasonable person who shared not only his physical circumstances but also his past history, his current beliefs, and various other aspects of his psychological makeup, would have acted as he did. But if the Donovan–Wildman argument already *assumes* that any viable version of the reasonable-person test for moral responsibility must construe the agent's situation in subjective terms, then it can hardly be used to *prove* that the best version of the reason-able-person test for moral responsibility must be subjective. Thus, if anyone did try to extend the argument in this way, he would simply end up moving in a circle.[14]

III

Because the legal literature supports neither an objective nor a subject-ive interpretation of the reasonable-person standard as it pertains to moral and prudential responsibility, we will have to decide between those interpretations in some other way. But is there any principled reason (beyond the fact that my account of these forms of responsibility will not work if we take an agent's situation to include too many psychological facts about him) to favor the objective interpretation?

I think, in fact, that there is; but before we can see what it comes to, we will have to shift our emphasis slightly. Up to now, I have repre-sented the choice as one that concerns our interpretation of the agent's situation. However, in this context, "situation" and "agent" are simply correlative terms that exhaustively partition certain facts. To say that a given fact is part of an agent's situation, or that it is external to him, is

14. Because Donovan and Wildman's argument against adopting an objective version of the reasonable-person standard in the legal context rests on their assumption that the moral version of the standard should also be subjective, any successful demonstration that the moral version of the standard should be objective would undermine their legal argument. In what follows, I will attempt to provide just such a demonstration.

simply to locate it on one side of the partition, while to call that same fact a part of the agent's makeup, or to say that it is internal to him, is to locate it on the other. The correlative nature of these terms suggests that instead of taking the dispute to concern the scope of the agent's situation, we could with equal justice take it to concern the dimensions of the agent himself. And, indeed, there is an obvious respect in which the latter representation is the more perspicuous; for because our larger topic is the epistemic condition for moral and prudential responsibility, it is clearly the bearer of those forms of responsibility—that is, the agent and not his situation—in whom we are primarily interested.

This shift in emphasis immediately opens up new possibilities. When we ask which facts about an agent we should take his situation to encompass, we find it hard to give a principled answer because there is no body of theory about the situations of agents upon which we can draw. However, and in stark contrast, there is a thriving if disorderly body of theory about the nature of agents themselves. This suggests that the way to make progress in determining on which side of the boundary to locate a person's beliefs, desires, dispositions, and traits is to seek our answer in precisely that body of theory.

When we do, we immediately find much that supports the objective approach; for when philosophers ask what makes someone the person he is, they very often appeal to some combination of his desires, beliefs, dispositions, and traits. I think that most philosophers (and most nonphilosophers) would readily affirm that these aspects of a person are among the determinants of his identity in a way that his physical attributes and social circumstances are not. There is of course disagreement about *how much* of a person's psychological makeup has this status—it is unclear, for example, whether urges and traits that an agent disavows or wishes not to have are thereby rendered external to his real or "core" self—but few would deny that traits such as blindness and physical infirmity are external in a way that many psychological features are not. This suggests that many philosophers would draw the line between an agent and his situation at about the same place as the traditional legal rule.

Whether or not this breezy speculation is correct, the question of where to draw that line is clearly a variant of the question of where to locate the boundaries of the responsible self. Not coincidentally, this last question is just the one that we must answer if we are to ascertain which psychological states are constitutive of an agent in the sense that PEC's condition (2b) requires. Moreover, for any given agent, the range of answers that exclude from his situation the psychological states that account for his failure to recognize his act as wrong or foolish will roughly coincide with the range of answers that construe those psychological states as constitutive of him. This suggests that the two requirements of PEC's second disjunct—that the agent's failure to respond to his evidence that his act is wrong or foolish be both (a) defective relative to the standards that determine what a reasonable person in his situation would realize and (b) traceable to his own constitutive attitudes and dispositions—are connected at a deep level. Although they appear distinct, the two requirements are rooted in a single theory of the responsible self.

And, because they are, I need not produce an independent argument that the psychological states whose interaction prevents agents from realizing that they are acting wrongly or foolishly are generally not elements of their situations. Instead, if I can show that those attitudes and traits are generally constitutive of their possessors, as PEC's condition (2b) requires, then the conclusion that they are not elements of their possessors' situations, as the preferred interpretation of its condition (2a) requires, will immediately follow. In the next chapter, I will argue that the relevant attitudes and traits are indeed constitutive of their possessors in precisely this way.

However, before I can make that argument, I must say something about the other unresolved question about PEC's condition (2a). This, it will be recalled, was the question of whether the standards that determine what a particular wrongdoer or foolish agent should be aware of, or what a reasonable person in his situation would be aware of, are genuinely normative or merely statistical. Unlike our first question about the standards that determine what agents should be aware of, this one does seem genuinely independent of the way we interpret condition (2b). For this reason, it will require separate treatment.

IV

At first glance, the case for a statistical interpretation of the standards that determine what agents in particular situations should be aware of may seem quite strong; for when we try to ascertain whether those standards have been met, we rely heavily on our beliefs about what others in similar situations generally *are* aware of. When we judge that Alessandra and Ryland should have realized what they were doing, our main rationale appears to be that most pet owners do not forget the animals that depend on them and that most raconteurs are sensitive to the sensitivities of their audience. Along similar lines, we would withdraw our judgment that Father Poteet should have realized that he lacked the space to merge if we discovered that enough other motorists who entered the freeway from the same ramp caused similar levels of carnage. Because our judgments about what any given agent should be aware of are so strongly influenced by our beliefs about what most others in that agent's (objective) situation *are* aware of, it may seem obvious that the standards that underlie those judgments are merely statistical.[15]

But, on closer inspection, this is not obvious at all; for even if the relevant standards are ones that most people can and do meet, it hardly follows that those standards apply only *because* most people can or do meet them. It is notoriously fallacious to infer, from the fact that each species occupies its own ecological niche, that each niche was created so the relevant species could fill it. We would commit a similar fallacy if we were to infer, from the fact that most people satisfy the standards in terms of which the reasonable person is defined, that those standards are

---

15. Some legal theorists have sought to differentiate the reasonable person from the average person on the grounds that the average person has occasional lapses which the reasonable person by definition never has; see, for example, A. P. Herbert, *Uncommon Law* (London: Methuen, 1935), and "The Reasonable Man of Negligence Law: A Health Report on the 'Odious Creature'," Osborne M. Reynolds, Jr., *Oklahoma Law Review* 23 (1970), 410–30. This distinction will preserve the statistical interpretation of what is reasonable as long as the level of responsiveness to evidence that the reasonable person is defined as invariably achieving is set by the level achieved on average by his less consistent actual counterparts. Among legal theorists, this last thesis appears to be widely influential— see, for example, Holmes, *The Common Law*, and George P. Fletcher, "A Theory of Criminal Negligence: A Comparative Analysis," *The University of Pennsylvania Law Review* 119 (January 1971), 401–38—and given the law's pragmatic aims, that seems entirely reasonable. However, because our current aims are so different, the reasoning that leads legal theorists to adopt this version of the statistical interpretation will again fail to carry over.

set where they are because, or so that, most people can satisfy them. The obvious alternative is that the standards are set independently, and that the fact that most people routinely meet them merely indicates that most people are the sorts of creatures to whom the concept of responsibility in fact applies.

Because this possibility remains open, we must examine the competing approaches on their merits. Moreover, when we do, we find good reason to reject the statistical approach. To see this, let us first revisit one of our examples—*Hot Dog* will do nicely—this time against a backdrop in which the general level of cognitive functioning has declined markedly. We may suppose, for example, that an epidemic of Alzheimer's has brought a drastic decrease in people's short-term memories and ability to retrieve what they know, or that some environmental pollutant has caused a widespread decline in people's cognitive functioning (as the lead in the drinking cups of the ancient Romans is said to have done). If such a shift has occurred, but if Alessandra is among the few who have managed to avoid the damage (perhaps because she drinks only bottled water), then the statistical and nonstatistical interpretations of the standards that determine what agents should be aware of will yield very different verdicts about her. On the statistical interpretation, the fact that most other people would also have forgotten about Sheba will imply that Alessandra's failure to remember the dog is not subpar, and hence that it is not the case that she should have remembered. By contrast, on a nonstatistical interpretation, the fact that most others would also have forgotten will imply neither of these things. In fact, the supposed general decline in cognitive functioning would clearly *not* alter our judgment that the unimpaired Alessandra should have realized that Sheba was stuck in the hot car. Thus, the norms that underlie such judgments cannot be based simply on statistics about what people generally realize.[16]

Taken by itself, this example does not discredit all versions of the statistical approach. Because the example turns on the fact that Alessandra herself is unimpaired, it remains possible to maintain that

---

16. Compare John Doris: "The determination of whether a person manifested reasonable ethical awareness should not be determined by reference to the frequency with which failures of awareness occur" (John Doris, *Lack of Character* [Cambridge: Cambridge University Press, 2002], 138).

the standard below which she has fallen is the one that is set by *her own* previous level of performance. It may be suggested, in other words, that the real import of the claim that Alessandra should have been aware of Sheba's plight is simply that this is the sort of thing that Alessandra generally does recognize. However, although this proposal has some initial credibility, a further variant of *Hot Dog* suggests that it, too, is inadequate. To bring out the difficulty, let us now suppose that Alessandra's exemption from the prevailing affliction was only temporary, and that she has recently become just as impaired as her fellows. If this is so, and if Alessandra forgets about Sheba very shortly after becoming impaired, then her failure to recognize the dog's plight will fall well below her previous level of performance. Hence, if the standard that determines what someone should be aware of is set by that person's own history of performance, then we will have to say that the newly impaired Alessandra should have realized that Sheba was stuck in the hot car. Because we clearly would not say this, the individualized statistical interpretation is evidently no more adequate than its nonindividualized counterpart.

This last variant shows that what matters about Alessandra is not what she has remembered in the past, but only what she is capable of remembering now. It therefore suggests the possibility of abandoning the statistical approach in favor of the view that the standards that govern what a person should realize at a given time are set precisely by that person's current cognitive capacities. Although the notion of a capacity is notoriously slippery, it seems possible to make sense of the claim that the original Alessandra was capable of remembering Sheba when she in fact forgot by appealing to some combination of (a) counterfactuals about what she would then have remembered under alternative conditions and (b) claims about the physical mechanisms of memory. Michael Smith proposes an account of just this sort when he writes that in order to determine whether someone has the capacity to form a certain belief that is supported by her evidence, we must

> abstract away from all those properties that could have an effect on what she believes except the relevant properties of her brain, and we must then ask whether a whole raft of counterfactuals are true of her. Would she have formed a whole host of similar beliefs in response to similar evidence? If she would have, then the suggestion is, assuming

that there is relevant structure in what underlies the truth of those counterfactuals, we can triangulate to the conclusion that, in the same nearby region of logical space, that same woman forms the right belief in response to the evidence she in fact considers. If all this is so, then it follows that she has the capacity to form the right belief in response to the evidence she in fact considers.[17]

Although Smith's woman, unlike Alessandra, is aware of the considerations that support the belief that she has failed to form, his account can easily be extended to cover a case in which she is not. Assuming that some such account can be made to work, and setting aside the complication that the relevant capacities are likely to come in degrees, let us now consider the possibility that the standards that determine what an agent in a given evidential situation should be aware of are set precisely by that agent's current cognitive capacities.

This proposal offers some definite advantages. For one thing, it allows us to make sense not only of our original judgments that Alessandra, Julian, and the others should have been aware of their acts' wrong-making features, but also of our judgments about what each agent should be aware of in each possible variant of each case. In addition, by relativizing what each agent should be aware of to his own cognitive capacities, the proposal avoids the implication that PEC's second disjunct is satisfied even by the severely retarded and the insane. Although the mental makeup of such persons can indeed be expected to cause them not to realize that they are acting wrongly or foolishly, their failure to realize this will never be substandard as long as the relevant standards are set by their own deficient cognitive capacities. Moreover, by taking the standards that determine what each agent should be aware of to be set entirely by that agent's own capacities, we will also satisfy the requirement that no one's responsibility should depend on any facts about anyone else. It is true that if what each agent should be aware of is determined exclusively by his own cognitive capacities, the relevant "shoulds" will not be robustly normative. However, if the proposal is otherwise defensible, then this implication is one we can simply accept.

---

17. Michael Smith, "Rational Capacities," in his *Ethics and the A Priori* (Cambridge: Cambridge University Press, 2004), 126.

V

But, in fact, the current proposal is *not* otherwise defensible. To see why, and thus to appreciate what the relevant standards really involve, we must consider one final round of variations on our examples.

Let us return to the original version of *Hot Dog*. On the proposed account, the Alessandra of that version should have realized that Sheba was in the car because she had just seen Sheba there and, being normal, she had the capacity to remember what she saw. But now let us add that Sheba was not the only thing that Alessandra saw—that when she cleared the backseat before leaving the car, she also saw an umbrella, last summer's beach novel, several fast-food wrappers, and Sheba's pull toy. Having seen these things at the same time that she saw Sheba, she must have been just as capable of remembering them as she was of remembering the dog. Thus, if what Alessandra should have remembered when she was in the school depends entirely on what she was then capable of remembering, then it must be just as true that she should have remembered Sheba's pull toy as it is that she should have remembered Sheba. Since in fact it is not the case that Alessandra should have remembered Sheba's pull toy—why should she?—the standards that underlie our judgments about what agents in particular epistemic situations should be aware of cannot be set exclusively by those agents cognitive capacities.

What is the difference between Sheba and her toy that makes it true that Alessandra should have remembered the one but not the other? When the question is put this way, the obvious answer is "Alessandra's obligations." A bit less cryptically, the reason Alessandra should have remembered Sheba is that she was under an obligation to protect the dog that she could not fulfill without remembering where the dog was; while the reason it is not the case that she should have remembered the toy is that she was under no corresponding obligation to do anything with or for it. Generalizing from this, we may conclude that what any given agent should recognize depends not merely on what that agent has the capacity to recognize given his evidence, but also on what he must recognize if he is to discharge his moral or prudential duties.

This is, I think, a significant result; for it suggests that there is an internal connection between the standards that determine what agents in specific epistemic situations should be aware of and the ostensibly quite different standards that determine what those agents morally and prudentially ought to do. It suggests, in other words, that the former "shoulds," which on the surface seem purely epistemic, are in fact rooted in the "oughts" of morality and prudence. This suggestion, if it can be sustained, will explain why the standards that determine what a given agent should realize seem more robustly normative than they would be if they merely recorded the agent's capacities.

However, before we can accept the suggestion, we must consider the objection that the standards of morality and prudence are practical while the standards of recognition are not. Because morality and prudence are action-guiding—because the central question to which they provide answers is "What should I do"—it may be thought that any secondary requirements to which they give rise must be action-guiding too. If morality and prudence govern only actions, and if they are the sources of the standards that determine what agents should be aware of, then it must be the case either that becoming aware of something is itself an action or that those standards call only for actions aimed at *acquiring* the relevant forms of awareness. However, of these alternatives, neither is at all plausible. The first is belied by the fact that becoming aware is not something we do but something that happens to us—not an action but a gift or a form of grace—while the second falls short because even someone who does everything he can to make himself aware of all morally and prudentially relevant considerations may still fail to realize something he should. Thus, if morality and prudence can give rise only to standards that dictate actions, then the standards that determine what agents should be aware of cannot be among those to which morality and prudence give rise.

But does this objection really show that the standards that determine what agents should be aware of cannot be importantly connected to the requirements of morality and prudence? Despite initial appearances, I think it does not. The problem is not merely that the objection tendentiously ignores the claim, advanced by many virtue ethicists, that the action-guiding requirements of morality are themselves derivative from deeper ideals of character that are *not* action-guiding.[18] It is, as

18. For lucid defense of this approach, see Rosalind Hursthouse, *On Virtue Ethics* (Oxford: Oxford University Press, 1999).

well, that even if we do not accept any form of virtue ethics, we must at least agree that morality undergirds the non-action-guiding standards by which we *assess* ideals of character. Traits such as honesty and kindness are not actions but remain virtues that people ought to have, and their having this status is surely bound up with morality's requiring that we act kindly and honestly. In addition, and relatedly, although feelings such as pride and attitudes such as indifference are not actions, morality can plausibly be said to require that we not take pride in wrongdoing or remain indifferent to injustice. Because the standards in terms of which we assess people's traits, feelings, and attitudes clearly *are* offshoots of our moral scheme, it is evidently possible for the demands of an action-guiding morality to ramify in many non-action-guiding directions. And, because of this, there can be no principled objection to the claim that those demands also extend to nonactional states of awareness.

VI

We are therefore free to conclude that the standards that determine what a given agent should be aware of are a joint function of (a) that agent's cognitive capacities, and (b) the moral and prudential requirements that apply to him. But how, exactly, might these factors fit together? How might an agent's cognitive capacities interact with the requirements of morality and prudence to give rise to the standards of awareness that apply to him?

In many familiar contexts, there is a clear distinction between the possession of a capacity and the choice to exercise it. So, for example, the reason I am not now running a ten minute mile is that although I have the capacity to do this, I have not chosen to exercise that capacity. By contrast, the reason I am not now running a *two* minute mile is that I lack the capacity and so have no choice in the matter. Taking our cue from this, we may be tempted to think of the requirements of morality and prudence as interacting with the cognitive capacities of the agents to whom they apply as follows: morality and prudence demand that agents become aware of any morally or prudentially relevant facts for which they have evidence, but these demands are weakened or cancelled when the agents lack the relevant cognitive capacities because someone who lacks a capacity cannot (effectively) choose to exercise it.

But, whatever else is true, this account cannot be correct; for because remembering, recognizing, and becoming aware are not actions at all, it follows that even when someone *is* fully capable of remembering, recognizing, and becoming aware of things, he cannot effectively choose when to exercise these capacities. To say that someone was capable of remembering something he forgot is only to say that he would have remembered it in an appropriate range of alternative situations; and exercising this capacity is never a matter of choice. Also, of course, if we did construe the cognitive capacities as ones that their possessors can choose to exercise, then we would have ushered the searchlight view out the front door only to see it reenter through the back.

Because no one can choose when to exercise his cognitive capacities, there remains a question about why the agents with these capacities are subject to higher standards of awareness than agents who lack them. If the statement that someone has a given cognitive capacity is made true exclusively by what he would be aware of in various non-actual situations, then why should that statement's truth have any bearing on what he should be aware of in the actual situation? Even if a normal unwitting wrongdoer would have realized that he was acting wrongly in most other circumstances while an impaired unwitting wrongdoer would not, why does it follow that the normal unwitting wrongdoer, but not the impaired one, should have realized that he was acting wrongly in the situation that actually prevailed?

To answer these questions, and thus complete our discussion of the standards that determine what agents should be aware of, we must remind ourselves of certain facts about the relevant cognitive capacities and certain related facts about the demands of morality and prudence. Where the cognitive capacities are concerned, the crucial fact is that their possession is a necessary condition for reason-responsiveness. To be a person who forms his beliefs and makes his decisions on the basis of the reasons his situation provides, an agent must be broadly disposed, among other things, to notice various features of his surroundings, to separate what is relevant from what is not, to preserve any relevant beliefs in his short-term memory, to retrieve information from his long-term memory as needed, and to draw the appropriate conclusions from his beliefs and goals. As a collectivity, these dispositions undergird both theoretical and practical rationality. And, correlatively, where morality and prudence are concerned, the crucial fact is that their demands address us precisely in our capacity *as* reason-responders. As we noted in chapter 4, what sets the demands of morality and prudence apart from other potential influences on our thought and action is just that they seek to move us to act by giving us good reasons to do so.

Taken together, these facts suggest a straightforward explanation of the connection between an agent's cognitive capacities and the standards that determine what he should be aware of. From the premises that the demands of morality and prudence are directed at agents in their capacity as reason-responders and that agents cannot be reason-responders if they lack the relevant cognitive capacities, we may conclude that the demands of morality and prudence are directed only at those who possess the relevant cognitive capacities, but not at those who lack them. This means that if the standards that determine what an agent should be aware of are offshoots *of* the demands of morality and prudence, then those standards cannot apply to agents who lack the relevant cognitive capacities either. However, why the standards of awareness are set higher for those who possess the relevant cognitive capacities than for those who lack them is precisely what we need to explain. Thus, to provide the needed explanation, it seems sufficient to point out that the cognitive capacities in question are among the enabling conditions for the applicability of the demands of morality and prudence themselves.

EIGHT

THE RESPONSIBLE SELF

How, if Alessandra, Julian, and the others have not consciously chosen either to act wrongly or to risk failing to realize that they are doing so, can the wrongness of their acts be attributable to them in a strong enough sense to render them responsible? The answer, I have suggested, is that even if each agent's failure to realize what he should is neither an action nor the foreseeable result of one, it may still have originated in him in the sense of resulting from the interaction of the very attitudes, dispositions, and traits that make him the person he is. To complete my defense of PEC, I must now argue for the conception of the responsible self that underlies this suggestion.

I

Even if our choices are not always causally determined, our failures to realize and remember things surely are. Thus, it is hardly controversial to say that whenever someone fails to realize what he should realize, or forgets what he should remember, his cognitive lapse can be traced to some combination of elements of his psychology and/or physiology. The harder question, though, is why this fact should have any bearing on the agent's responsibility. Why should our ability to trace a person's cognitive lapse to the effects of certain subpersonal states have anything to do with our reactions to *him*?

To answer this question, I will have to show that a person's causally effective subpersonal states are so closely related *to* him that it is reasonable to view the cognitive failures to which they give rise—and so, by extension, the ensuing wrong or foolish acts—as originating *in* him. I will have to show, in other words, that the relevant subpersonal states are, in some suitable sense, among the person's constitutive features. The task of showing this is complicated by the fact that terms like "constitutive feature" and "feature that makes someone the person he is" are multiply ambiguous, and can be used to designate anything from a feature that is part of someone's metaphysical essence to one that is central to his self-image. However, because our guiding aim is to understand the conditions under which agents can be held responsible for what they do, the obvious way to sidestep these ambiguities is to allow the relevant conception of the self to be shaped by intellectual pressures that originate in the concept of responsibility itself. As we will see, these intellectual pressures are generated mainly by facts we have already encountered. They arise because only beings that are capable of acting for reasons can qualify as responsible, because each reason-responder is both embodied and endowed with a subjectivity that is associated with a unique perspective, and because those who hold agents responsible typically do not share either their subjectivity or the perspectives they occupied when they acted.

How, in light of such facts, should we think of the responsible self? To get an initial sense of the possibilities, let us begin by considering two extreme positions, one maximalist and the other minimalist. The maximalist position identifies the responsible self with the whole human organism. It denies that any of an agent's physical or psychological features are any more constitutive of him than any others, and so insists that every (skin-in) fact about him, from his height or his white blood count through his most deeply held values, is equally part of what makes him the person he is.[1] By contrast, the minimalist position takes

---

1. The importance of the physical boundaries of the human organism has been challenged both on the grounds that the contents of beliefs are partially determined by external events and on the grounds that external events play an active role in driving cognitive processes; see, respectively, Tyler Burge, "Individualism and the Mental," *Midwest Studies in Philosophy* 4 (1979), 73–122, and Andy Clark and David Chalmers,

its cue from the fact that many types of entity—stones, animals, and infants, for example—cannot be responsible for anything at all. Because responsibility evidently requires features that such entities lack, the minimalist reasons that any adequate theory of the responsible self must focus exclusively on these. This leads him to abstract away from all merely physical aspects of the person, and to view responsible selves as constituted entirely by characteristics such as rationality or conscious will.

Although both extreme positions embody important insights, I want to argue that neither is adequate. Where the maximalist position is concerned, the problem is obvious: although each responsible agent is of course a human being, and so is located in the natural world and is subject to its causal laws, the vast majority of each human's physical features (and perhaps also many of his psychological features) have no obvious connection to any of his beliefs about himself or the world, his judgments about what he has reason to believe or do, or his actual decisions, actions, and omissions. When a given physical or psychological feature is this dissociated from all the aspects of its possessor's life which alone make questions of responsibility meaningful, there is simply no reason to view it either as any part of what makes him a responsible agent or, *a fortiori*, as any part of what makes him the particular responsible agent he is.

Because an indiscriminately inclusive approach would draw the boundaries of the responsible self far too broadly, we must draw back from the maximalist position. But how far back should we draw? Given the wide consensus that any being that entirely lacked consciousness, or that sometimes or always had it but was systematically insensitive to theoretical or practical reasons, would not qualify as a responsible agent,[2] there is an obvious case for taking consciousness and reason-responsiveness to fall within the boundaries of the responsible self. The

"The Extended Mind," *Analysis*, 58 (1998), 10–23. If either challenge can be sustained, then there is room for a supermaximalist position according to which the responsible self is constituted by all of the agent's skin-in features *and more*.

2. For example, Thomas Scanlon—no friend of the searchlight view—has observed that "it is crucial to a creature's being a rational creature that conscious judgment is one factor affecting its behavior" (Thomas Scanlon, *What We Owe to Each Other* [Cambridge, MA: Harvard University Press, 1998], 282).

harder question, though, is which other features of human beings fall within those boundaries. If we answer "none," and abstract away from everything about the responsible agent *except* his consciousness or reason-responsiveness, then we will have arrived at the minimalist position.

Because so many reason-based choices are conscious, it may at first seem that any minimalist must take responsible agents to be constituted by both consciousness *and* reason-responsiveness. However, the issue is complicated by the fact that consciousness and reason-responsiveness can themselves come apart. It is quite possible to be a conscious chooser without being reason-responsive; and, as we saw in chapter 4, it is also possible to respond to reasons at a nonconscious level. Because consciousness and reason-responsiveness need not coincide, there is room for versions of minimalism which take responsible agents to be constituted exclusively by their capacity for conscious choice, exclusively by their reason-responsiveness, or by both together.

The distinction between accounts that represent responsible selves as conscious choosers and those that represent them as reason-responders is far from trivial. It is precisely this distinction that underlies the contrast between the variant of the searchlight view that Neil Levy labels "volitionism"—the view that "an agent is responsible for something (an act, omission, attitude, and so on) just in case that agent has—directly or indirectly—*chosen* that thing"[3]—and the influential opposing view, espoused by Thomas Scanlon and Angela Smith and often labeled "attributionism," which asserts that agents are responsible for all of the actions, beliefs, and attitudes, conscious or not, that reflect their judgments about what they have reason to do, believe, or feel.[4] Because volitionism abstracts away from everything except an agent's conscious choices, it in effect identifies the responsible self with, or in

3. Neil Levy, "The Good, the Bad, and the Blameworthy," *Journal of Ethics and Social Philosophy* 1 (June 2005), 2.

4. Scanlon endorses this view at various places in *What We Owe to Each Other*. Angela Smith affirms it in a series of articles including "Responsibility for Attitudes: Activity and Passivity in Mental Life," *Ethics* 115 (January 2005), 236–71, "Conflicting Attitudes, Moral Agency, and Conceptions of the Self," *Philosophical Topics* 32 (Spring and Fall 2004), 331–52, and "Control, Responsibility, and Moral Assessment," *Philosophical Studies* 138 (April 2008), 367–92.

terms of, the first-person perspective from which he views the world. By contrast, because attributionism abstracts away from everything except an agent's judgments about reasons, it in effect identifies responsible selves with their capacity to reach such judgments.

Given the intimate connections between responsibility on the one hand and consciousness and reason-responsiveness on the other, both minimalist views clearly satisfy the requirement that responsible selves be constituted exclusively by features that have some important bearing on their responsibility. However, importantly, it is also possible to satisfy this requirement in ways that are less ruthlessly minimal. We will also satisfy it if we take each responsible self to be constituted not merely by his consciousness or reason-responsiveness, but also by certain physical or mental features to which consciousness and reason-responsiveness are themselves intimately linked. By thus working outward from these core features, we can identify a whole array of conceptions that stand between the maximalist and minimalist extremes. Although many of these intermediate possibilities need not concern us, there is one addition to the minimalist view that I think is definitely required. In what follows, I will first propose, and then defend, an account that incorporates that addition.

II

Put baldly and without defense, my basic idea is that a responsible agent is best identified not only with his subjectivity or rationality but also with their causes. Put a bit more specifically, what I will argue is that we should think of each responsible agent not merely as a conscious center of will, nor yet as an entity that attempts to evaluate its practical and theoretical reasons and to base its beliefs and actions on them, but rather as an enduring causal structure whose elements interact in ways that *give rise to* these responsibility-related activities. As a corollary, when I say that a given psychological or physiological state is among the constitutive features of a particular self, or that it is part of what makes him the person he is, what I will mean is simply that it is among the elements of the system whose causal interactions determine the contents of the conscious thoughts and deliberative activities in whose absence he would not qualify as responsible at all.

As so understood, each responsible agent's constitutive features will be quite extensive. It is a commonplace that each person's theoretical and practical decisions are influenced by factors such as his background beliefs, his moral commitments, his views about what is good and valuable, and what he notices and finds salient. His decisions are influenced, as well, by his degree of optimism or pessimism, his attitude toward risk, and many other facets of his emotional makeup. Hence, by my account, all such features of an agent will qualify as constitutive. In addition, as long as they remain compatible with the general framework of folk psychology within which the notions of agency, reasons, and responsibility are embedded, we can expect that many of the factors that explain an agent's thoughts and actions at other, deeper levels—the relevant neurophysiological mechanisms, for example, or the functionally defined constructs that populate the flow charts of cognitive psychologists—will qualify as constitutive too. As I hope is obvious, these claims are meant to imply not that we cannot classify someone as a responsible self without being able to *identify* the relevant causal structures, but only that in so classifying him, we assume that such structures do in fact exist.

Because my proposal identifies each responsible agent with whatever psychological and physical structures sustain his normal patterns of intellectual functioning, it is clearly a variant of the familiar view that the identity of each such agent is determined by his character. It is, however, quite different from the familiar versions of this view that understand character exclusively in terms of behavioral or affective dispositions, deeply held value-commitments, or the relations between the agent's higher- and lower-order attitudes. What sets my approach to character apart from these—and, not coincidentally, what promises to enable it to play the role that PEC assigns it—is of course its frankly causal nature.

There is, however, a question about its ability to fulfill this promise. Put most simply, the difficulty is that if we identify a responsible agent's constitutive features by working backward from his reason-responsive activities to their causes, then it is hard to see how we can take those same features to give rise to acts or omissions that are *not* reason-responsive. If what renders an element of someone's psychology constitutive is precisely its role in *sustaining* his rationality-related activities, then how can any feature by which he is constituted *prevent* him from engaging effectively in such activities? And, if this is not possible, then how can unwitting wrongdoers like Alessandra, Julian, and Scout be linked to their wrong acts by the fact that their failures to appreciate the acts' wrongness were caused by their constitutive features?

To answer these questions, and thus complete my sketch of the view that I am proposing, I want to make two points, one conceptual and one broadly empirical. The conceptual point is simply that there is no contradiction in the claim that a feature that is constitutive of an agent in the specified sense can sometimes prevent him from responding to reasons. As long as the effects of any given element of an organized psychological system depend both on that element's interplay with the system's other elements and on many external factors—and this, of course, is always the case—it will be quite possible for a state that generally contributes to its possessor's reason-responsiveness to interfere with it on a given occasion. We are all familiar with many normally but not invariably reliable systems—cars whose sparkplugs occasionally do not fire, for example, and computers that occasionally freeze—whose internal organization allows us to understand both why they are generally reliable and why they sometimes malfunction. Thus, if the current objection is to have bite, it will have to be because the aspects of the relevant agents' psychologies that explain their cognitive lapses do not in fact fit this description.

But why, exactly, should we suppose this? Why, when Alessandra forgets about Sheba because she is distracted by the dispute at the school, should we suppose that the aspects of her psychology that account for her distraction—her concern for her children, for example, or her tendency to focus intensely on whatever issue is at hand—are anything but consistent contributors to the way she characteristically approaches practical and theoretical problems? When Ryland fails to realize that the members of her audience will find her anecdote offensive, why view the self-absorption that explains her failure as anything other than an unremarkable (if sometimes distorting) member of the vast collection of attitudes whose interaction determines the usual shape of her judgments about reasons? Even when Joliet panics and Father Poteet misjudges the available road space, why exclude either her emotional makeup or the speed with which he processes visual cues from the factors that play a role in determining the contours of their respective judgments about reasons? As long as each of our nine agents surpasses the general threshold for reason-responsiveness, on what basis could we possibly distinguish the aspects of their psychology that help to sustain this happy state of affairs from those that do not?

III

I have proposed that we identify each agent with the collection of physical and psychological states whose elements interact to sustain his characteristic patterns of conscious and rational activity. If this proposal can be defended, it will provide PEC's condition (2b) with the theoretical backing it requires. However, I have not yet said anything about why we should adopt the proposal, and so my next task is to provide the needed defense. Put most simply, my strategy will be to argue that each more minimal conception is subject to various difficulties which are best resolved by augmenting it with a causal component.

Let us begin with the version of minimalism that focuses exclusively on the responsible agent's subjectivity. Because each person is responsible only for his own actions, and because each person's decisions reflect his own view of his situation, it is quite natural to base our conception of the responsible self on the picture that each of us has of himself when he deliberates. Moreover, although Hume was right to observe that we never encounter the bearer of our thoughts, but only their contents, when we introspect,[5] we nevertheless cannot help thinking of ourselves (and so by analogy others) as standing apart from our thoughts and choosing among the options they present. Thus, if we take as our point of departure the responsible agent's own perspective on the world, we will naturally think of such agents as simple conscious centers of will.

But *should* we take the first-person perspective as our point of departure? Doubts arise when we remind ourselves that the concept of responsibility is itself interpersonal. As we saw in chapter 3, we judge that others are responsible at least as often as we render such judgments about ourselves. Because any adequate account of the responsible self must make sense of both sorts of judgments, our concept of the

---

5. David Hume, *Treatise of Human Nature*, ed. L. A. Selby-Bigge (Oxford: Oxford University Press, 1960), book I, sec. VI, part IV.

responsible self must allow us to think of other selves from our own perspective rather than theirs. This does not mean that another's perspective cannot play a role in the way we think of him—it is perfectly possible for me to acknowledge that you have a perspective, and that things seem a certain way to you from it, from my own quite different perspective—but it does mean that we must be able to think of the other without actually *occupying* his perspective.[6] Because no one has access to anyone else's subjectivity, any account that identified each responsible self with his own subjectivity would not be truly interpersonal. By contrast, we will have little difficulty understanding how responsibility can be interpersonal if we identify each responsible self with the *causes* of his subjectivity; for to gain access to these causes, we need not actually occupy the other's point of view, but need only hold reasonable beliefs about its existence and contents.

A further (and closely related) problem with the first-personal approach is that it does not locate responsible selves *in the world*. If we adopted that approach, and viewed each responsible self as constituted exclusively by his subjectivity, then our conception of such selves would be entirely nonempirical. Because each person's consciousness is his alone, its particulars are not knowable through the methods of any branch of psychology, folk or experimental, or of any of the physical sciences. By contrast, an account that identifies responsible selves with causally effective psychological structures is, at least in principle, responsive to evidence about the nature of the causally operative states. Because it allows us to introduce such evidence, such an account is suitably interpersonal. For this reason, the third-person approach seems more able than its first-personal rival to integrate the moral notion of responsibility into a broadly naturalistic picture of the world.

Even by themselves, these considerations tell heavily against construing responsible selves simply as conscious centers of will. However, the case against that view becomes even more compelling when we turn from the reasons not to privilege the first-person perspective to a careful

---

6. Even if we accept the Nagelian fantasy of full identification with another's perspective, all that we can take it to involve is an accurate reconstruction of the contents of the other's perspective from our own perspective. Even when I imagine what it's like to be another, it's still me who is doing the imagining.

examination of what that perspective actually involves; for far from compelling us to think of ourselves as constituted exclusively by our own subjectivity, the first-person perspective actually gives us reason to move toward, if not all the way to, a view of ourselves that is much like the one I am defending. To bring out the aspects of the first-person perspective that press us to think of ourselves as constituted partly by causally effective psychological structures, I will begin by briefly revisiting a short stretch of my own recent mental history.

Earlier this morning, when I sat down to write, I did so with the aim of illustrating my claim that our experience as practical agents points to aspects of us that are hidden from consciousness, but I didn't yet have any particular examples in mind. But why, if I viewed myself simply as a conscious center of will, should I have had any expectation of finding suitable examples of which I was not yet aware? Why was I so confident that I could come up with what I needed? The answer, as I now reconstruct it, is partly that I was counting on tapping into the residue of thought that had been deposited in the months when my mind had circled around different ways of developing the book's later argument— a residue of whose exact contents I was at the moment unaware, but of whose existence I was nevertheless certain—and partly that experience has taught me to trust my mind's ability to generate new thoughts more or less on cue. However, to whatever extent my intention rested on the assumption that my previous animadversions had left traces that were not currently before my consciousness, I must, in forming it, have regarded myself as having dimensions that neither were illuminated by the searchlight of my consciousness nor were any part of the illuminative apparatus. Analogously, to whatever extent my intention rested on the assumption that my mind was capable of offering up new thoughts, I must, in forming it, have regarded myself as possessing generative capacities that are unrelated to my will. Thus, taken together, the two explanations of my confidence suggest that I must have viewed myself as far more than a conscious center of will.

This example is of course heavily autobiographical. Because of this, and also because the activity of writing philosophy is highly idiosyncratic, the example may appear to provide my position with only limited support. However, in fact, the example's details are there only to make it vivid. To generalize the point in a way that shows why practical agents can *never* view themselves simply as conscious centers of will, we need only remind ourselves of just how restricted the contents of *anyone's* consciousness are.

For even if we agree that those contents can include both what an agent is focusing on and what he is passively aware of—even if the driver who was introduced in Chapter 1 can simultaneously be conscious not only of the approaching exit that he is determined not to miss, but also of the car that is approaching on the left, the fact that he is slightly exceeding the speed limit, and his passenger's unfolding anecdote— these items still represent only the tiniest fraction of the information to which he must take himself to have access in order to carry out his task. If that driver is like most of us, then he is not thinking about any (let alone all) of the turns that he will have to make, or the mechanical operations that he will have to execute, in order to deliver his passenger safely to the airport; and still less is he rehearsing what he will do if he has a flat, if he encounters a traffic jam, if his passenger has a seizure, or if he finds himself in any of the other innumerable unexpected circum- stances that could conceivably arise. In each case, he simply trusts himself to think of what is needed when the time comes. No agent could function at all if he did not have confidence that his mind will, just of its own accord, dip into his memory bank to deliver up just the information he needs at just the time he needs it. However, if this reliance on what is available to us despite our not being conscious of it is built right into our practical deliberation (and, I might add, into our theoretical ratiocination) at every step of the way, then the conception of ourselves that informs our deliberation and ratiocination must itself have a substantial nonconscious dimension. This means that thinking of oneself exclusively as a conscious center of will is just about as coherent as thinking of oneself as a front with no back.

By unpacking the assumptions that make it possible to project our practical deliberations into the future, we arrive at a picture of the deliberating self that construes it as (*a*) containing a substantial non- conscious component, and (*b*) playing a causal role in generating the thoughts that rise to consciousness at different moments, and (*c*) gen- erally (though not invariably) functioning in ways that sustain our reason-related activities. In each respect, that picture is at worst consist- ent with, and at best highly suggestive of, the one I am defending. This means that even if we accept the dubious assumption that the best way to understand the nature of the responsible self is to rely on the picture of himself that each agent has when he deliberates, we will have little reason to accept, and much reason to reject, the view that responsible selves are simply conscious centers of will.

IV

The minimalist view of the self against which I have just argued has a long history. It is, for example, a recognizable descendant of Descartes' claim that he is simply a thinking thing. By contrast, my other minimalist target, which takes responsible agents to be constituted exclusively by their ability to form judgments about reasons, is less familiar and of more recent vintage. Thus, before I proceed to my argument, a bit of stage-setting is in order.

As I have said, I think a view of this sort is implicit in an influential approach to responsibility that has recently been developed by Thomas Scanlon and Angela Smith. Scanlon and Smith both maintain that agents are responsible for precisely those attitudes and actions that reflect their judgments about what they have reason to believe or do. They both maintain, as well, that many such "judgment-sensitive" attitudes and actions are not consciously chosen. In a passage that combines both points, Scanlon has written that

> The idea of judgment sensitivity helps to isolate the sense in which attitudes can be things we are "responsible for" even when, unlike most voluntary acts, they are not the result of choice or decision. Not only many perceptual beliefs, but many other attitudes as well arise in us unbidden, without conscious choice or decision. Nonetheless, as continuing states these attitudes are "up to us"—that is, they depend on our judgment as to whether appropriate reasons are present. Because of this dependence on judgment, these are things we can properly be "held responsible" for in several senses of that phrase: they can be properly attributed to us, and we can properly be asked to defend them—to justify the judgment they reflect.[7]

And Smith expresses the same combination of ideas when she writes:

---

7. Scanlon, *What We Owe to Each Other*, 21–22.

To say that an agent is morally responsible for some thing . . . is to say that that thing reflects her rational judgment in a way that makes it appropriate, in principle, to ask her to defend or justify it. . . . [M]ost of our desires, beliefs, and other attitudes seem to meet this condition of judgment-dependence, even though they do not commonly reflect a choice or decision, and are not normally under our voluntary control.[8]

It is because Scanlon and Smith restrict an agent's responsibility to those attitudes and actions that reflect his own judgments, and that in this sense can be attributed to him, that their position is known as attributionism.[9]

Although neither of the quoted passages explicitly mentions the responsible self, the obvious explanation of why Scanlon and Smith take an action's judgment-sensitivity to render the agent responsible for it is that they see each agent as standing in some especially close relation *to* his judgments about reasons. This makes it natural to interpret them as maintaining that it is precisely the ability to make such judgments that constitutes someone as a responsible agent, and that it is precisely the contents of a person's judgments that make him the particular responsible agent he is. This interpretation appears to be implicit in Neil Levy's assertion that "[o]n the attributionist account, I am responsible for my actions and omissions insofar as they express my identity as a practical agent,"[10] and Smith, at least, has said things that suggest that she would accept it.[11] In what follows, I shall accept it too.

8. Smith, "Control, Responsibility, and Moral Assessment," 369–370.

9. In his influential essay "Two Faces of Responsibility" (in his *Agency and Answerability* [Oxford: Oxford University Press, 2004]), Gary Watson distinguishes between responsibility as attributability and responsibility as accountability. Because an agent is responsible in the attributability sense when his act flows from, or expresses, his "evaluative commitments," the first of these notions is at least a close relative of the Scanlon–Smith view. Others who use the term "attributionism" to refer to that view include Neil Levy and Angela Smith herself.

10. Levy, "The Good, the Bad, and the Blameworthy," 4.

11. In particular, she comes close to endorsing it in "Character, Blameworthiness, and Blame: Comments on George Sher's *In Praise of Blame*," *Philosophical Studies* 137 (January 2008), 31–39. One of Smith's targets in that essay is the claim, advanced in my earlier book *In Praise of Blame* (Oxford: Oxford University Press, 2006), that what connects a wrongdoer to his bad act in a way that makes it reasonable to blame him for it is the causal connection that obtains between his desires, beliefs, and dispositions and the act's bad-making features. To this claim, Smith objects.

Like the claim that responsible agents are simply conscious centers of will, the claim that they are constituted by their ability to make judgments about reasons is vulnerable to certain objections that are best met by augmenting this view with a causal component. One such objection emerges when we try to square the attributionist's claim that an agent's responsibility is restricted to those features of his acts that reflect his judgments about reasons with the fact that agents often seem responsible for acts whose wrong-making features have not registered with them at all. So, for example, although Alessandra's extended stay in the school is backed by her judgment that she has good reason to hash things out with the authorities, the feature of her act that makes it wrong—the fact that she is leaving Sheba unattended in a hot car—plays no role at all in shaping this judgment. Because Alessandra has entirely forgotten about Sheba, the dog's plight does not enter her deliberation even as a countervailing consideration whose weight she takes into account but judges to be insufficient to sway her decision. However, if the wrong-making feature of what Alessandra does has no input at all into her all-things-considered judgment that she has reason to do it, then it is hard to see how that judgment can possibly connect her to the act's wrongness in a way that renders her responsible for it.

To deal with cases of this sort, those who restrict an agent's responsibility to those features of his acts that reflect his judgments about reasons sometimes point out that when an agent fails to notice a certain

> Why should *I* be blamed for the fact that some random collection of psychological states have causally interacted in my mental history in such a way as to produce a bad action? What do *I* have to do with any of that? (33)

Smith also writes that "we seem to have lost 'the agent' in all of this talk about the desires, beliefs, and dispositions that operate within him to produce his actions" (33) and that

> [i]n my view, the most plausible candidate for what it is that links an agent to his attitudes and dispositions—as well as to his intentional actions—is his *evaluative judgment*. . . . It is these judgments—judgments about what is good, worthwhile, or important—that in my view provide the crucial "link" between the agent and his attitudes and actions (34).

Taken together, these passages strongly suggest that Smith takes judgments about reasons to be relevant not only to the conditions under which we can attribute responsibility but also to the nature of the agents to whom we can attribute it.

feature of what he is doing, his cognitive failure may itself reflect a judgment that the relevant feature is not a significant source of reasons. Thus, to quote Angela Smith again:

> if one judges some thing or person to be important or significant in some way, this should (rationally) have an influence on one's tendency to notice factors which pertain to the existence, welfare, or flourishing of that thing or person. If this is so, then the fact that a person fails to take note of such factors in certain circumstances is at least some indication that she does not accept this evaluative judgment.[12]

Given the hedged nature of Smith's claim, I see no reason to disagree with it. However, precisely because the claim is so hedged, it does not rule out the possibility that there are also failures to notice morally relevant features of acts that are *not* themselves judgment-based. In particular, in Alessandra's case (and, I would argue, in many others), the urgency of the dispute, and its high emotional volume, seem by themselves to be quite sufficient to explain her failure to notice her act's wrong-making feature. Because the adequacy of this explanation would not block the conclusion that Alessandra is responsible for leaving Sheba in the car, the essential difficulty remains unresolved. To resolve it, we must locate the significance of Alessandra's failure to remember Sheba not in what it reveals about her judgments about reasons, but rather in its being caused by the same psychophysical structure that sustains her ability to *make* such judgments.

We can also bring out the need to augment attributionism with some sort of causal component in another way. In its most straightforward form, attributionism takes agents to be responsible for all and only those features of their attitudes and actions that reflect their judgments about reasons. However, when it is understood in this way, attributionism is *too* straightforward; for we can easily imagine agents whose actions, beliefs, and feelings are indeed grounded in their judgments about what they have reason to do, believe, and feel, yet whom no one would view as responsible for anything they do. To envision such a person, we need only imagine someone whose judgments about reasons are sufficiently capricious or

---

12. Smith, "Responsibility for Attitudes," 244.

unintelligible. Suppose, for example, that someone takes the fact that it is raining to be a reason to shave the left side of his head, the fact that the floor is not swept to be a reason to expect a financial windfall, and the fact that his cat's nose is running to be grounds for intense envy; and suppose, further, that these strange judgments are not backed by any further beliefs that are not equally implausible. Although this agent's actions, beliefs, and feelings will all be grounded in judgments about reasons, that will hardly qualify him as responsible; and the reason is clearly that his judgments about what he has reason to do, believe, and feel will bear no relation to what he *in fact* has reason to do, believe, and feel.

Because what makes this case problematic is the agent's inability to recognize his actual reasons, the obvious way for the attributionist to block the difficulty is to include that ability in the features that someone must have to be a responsible agent. Instead of taking responsible agents to be constituted by their ability to form judgments about what they have reason to do, believe, and feel, he must take them to be constituted by the more demanding ability to form *accurate* judgments about what they have reason to do, believe, and feel. If the need for this addition is not immediately apparent, it is probably because most of the judgment-sensitive attitudes and actions that we encounter are grounded in judgments about reasons that we can at least understand even if we do not share them. However, even if we rarely deal with agents whose judgments about reasons float entirely free of reality, the fact that such individuals can and do exist, and that we are definitely not inclined to regard them as responsible, makes it hard to see how any attributionist could resist some such addition.

But if the attributionist does *not* resist the addition, then he may also have to introduce a causal element into his account. The introduction of such an element may be necessary because it is hard to see how an agent's actual and counterfactual judgments about his reasons could systematically come out to be true without being causally dependent on whatever *makes* them true. If there were no causal relation between the agent's judgments about his reasons and their truth-makers, then the continuing actual and counterfactual accuracy of those judgments would simply be a miracle.[13] Because a capacity to reach accurate judgments about one's

---

13. Because this reasoning assumes nothing about the nature of a person's reasons, it is neutral between the view that the relevant truth-makers include aspects of his situation and the view that they consist solely of his other beliefs and/or desires.

reasons is only intelligible if we take it to have a causal basis, anyone who takes that capacity to be constitutive of responsible selves must be under heavy pressure to take its causal basis to be constitutive of them too.

And, because of this, the need to incorporate the capacity to recognize one's actual reasons will move attributionism much closer to my own account. The reason for the convergence is not just that the new attributionist claim that responsible agents must be capable of forming accurate judgments about their reasons will coincide with my own earlier own claim, advanced in chapter 7, that even someone whose failure to recognize that he is acting wrongly or foolishly is due to his constitutive psychology will not be responsible for acting that way unless he has the general capacity to draw the sorts of conclusions from his evidence that he did not draw on this occasion. It is, more deeply, that my broader account offers just the resources that are needed to capture the causal basis of any such capacity. Because I have proposed that we identify each responsible agent with whatever psychological or physical structure *gives rise to* his judgments about what he has reason to believe or do, I can build the accuracy requirement into my account by simply adding that any relevant structures must have causal properties that render the agents' judgments about reasons accurate within an appropriate range of actual and counterfactual situations. Indeed, because I originally identified the relevant causal structures by working backward from instances in which responsible agents *do* recognize and respond to their actual reasons, this requirement has been built into my account from the start. Thus, by following up on the need to tether the responsible agent's judgments about reasons to reality, we encounter yet a further reason to move in the direction of an account like mine.

V

To answer the linked questions of what makes someone a responsible agent and what makes someone the particular responsible agent he is, I have argued that we must look beyond the agent's consciousness and reason-responsiveness to the causal structures that sustain them. The resulting account is far more inclusive than the minimalist views which hold that what makes someone a responsible agent is simply his consciousness and/or reason-responsiveness and that what makes someone the particular responsible agent he is, is simply the contents of his consciousness and/or his judgments about reasons; but it is far less inclusive than the maximalist view that treats all facts about a responsible agent as equally constitutive of him. Mine is, however, far from the only account to occupy this intermediate territory, and so I must say something about its relation to its conceptual neighbors.

We can divide the most important of these into two broad groups, both of which also take responsible agents to be constituted by some but not all elements of their psychology, but which disagree about which elements are in and which are out. Put most simply, the difference is that one group draws the distinction synchronically while the other draws it diachronically. Views of the first sort, inspired by the influential work of Harry Frankfurt, take each responsible agent to be constituted by just those aspects of his character that he in some sense accepts. Philosophers who take this approach explicate the relevant form of acceptance in terms of factors such as wanting to have and be moved by one's lower-order desires, holding values that endorse or at least do not condemn those desires, identifying with certain attitudes while dissociating oneself from others, and being unable to avoid these forms of identification or dissociation.[14] By contrast, views of the second sort seek to exclude attitudes with objectionable causes such as manipulation, brainwashing, and certain forms of conditioning by restricting a responsible agent's constitutive features to those aspects of his character that have the right kind of causal history.[15]

To say that a responsible agent is constituted only by attitudes he accepts is not to say that he is constituted by *all* such attitudes, so we can easily combine versions of the two approaches. To do so, we need

14. Harry Frankfurt introduces this idea in his seminal essay "Freedom of the Will and the Concept of a Person," and explores it in a number of the other papers in his collection *The Importance of What We Care About* (Cambridge: Cambridge University Press, 1988). Two influential works that develop the idea in different ways are Gary Watson, "Free Agency," *The Journal of Philosophy* 72 (1975), 205–20, and Christine Korsgaard, *The Sources of Normativity* (Cambridge: Cambridge University Press, 1996), lecture 3.

15. See, for example, John Fischer and Mark Ravizza, *Responsibility and Control* (Cambridge: Cambridge University Press, 1988), chapter 7, and Alfred Mele, *Autonomous Agents* (Oxford: Oxford University Press, 1995).

only say that being accepted by the agent is one necessary condition for inclusion while having the right kind of history is another. Taking his cue from this, someone might be tempted to go further and combine versions of either or both accounts with my own. However, it is important to realize that, for simple logical reasons, this last option is not open.

To see why this is so, let us first consider the combination of my own account, which asserts that each responsible agent is constituted by the full set of psychological states whose interaction sustains his rationality-related activities, with the view that responsible agents are constituted only by those psychological states that they in some sense accept. If someone were to advance this combined account, then he would have to acknowledge that there could be a person for whom one and the same psychological state was both an element of the psychological structure that causally sustained his rationality-related activities, and thus was constitutive of him, but was also an aspect of his personality that he rejected, and thus was *not* constitutive of him. Because this conjunction is a straightforward contradiction, no combination of views that implies its possibility can be accepted. Moreover, because the set of psychological states that sustains an agent's rationality-related activities might well operate very differently, or might not operate at all, if we subtracted some of its elements, we cannot avoid the difficulty by stipulating that an agent's constitutive features consist only of whichever elements of the sustaining set he does *not* reject. Because of this, and because a similar contradiction would emerge if we tried to combine my own account with the view that a responsible agent is constituted only by that subset of his psychological states with the right kinds of histories, my account is clearly incompatible with each of its more famous alternatives.

Although this implication obviously raises the stakes, the escalation is not one by which I am particularly bothered; for neither alternative appears to me to be especially strongly motivated. Where the 'acceptance' view is concerned, the difficulty is partly that describing an agent's aversion to a hard-to-resist and destructive element of his personality in the language of alienation and otherness seems distorting and tendentious— isn't it at least as accurate to describe him as appalled that *he* is that way?— and partly that even the strongest feeling that a certain element of one's personality is alien or external just doesn't seem to be a very good basis upon which to conclude that it really is.[16] Where the right-kind-of-history view is concerned, the difficulty is that the simplest explanation of why those who were brainwashed, indoctrinated, and the like do not seem responsible is that they have been rendered incapable of responding to certain sorts of reasons—a fact that has nothing to do with their histories and everything to do with their current mental makeup.[17] These observations are of course the merest gestures at arguments, and I proffer them not as reasons to reject the views with which mine is incompatible, but only as explanations of why I am not bothered by the incompatibility. My reason for rejecting these views is the one I have already given—that by taking as our point of departure the consciousness and reason-responsiveness that responsibility undeniably presupposes, we are led to adopt the sort of causal account that rules them out.

16. For further criticism of this family of views, see Nomy Arpaly and Timothy Schroeder, "Praise, Blame, and the Whole Self," *Philosophical Studies* 93 (1999), 161–88, and Susan Wolf, *Freedom Within Reason* (Oxford: Oxford University Press, 1990), chapter 2.

17. See, in this connection, Susan Wolf, "Sanity and the Metaphysics of Responsibility," in Ferdinand David Schoeman, ed., *Responsibility, Character, and the Emotions: New Essays in Moral Psychology* (Cambridge: Cambridge University Press, 1988), 46–62.

NINE

OUT OF CONTROL

At the end of Chapter 6, I remarked that given the searchlight view's unacceptable implications, the real question was not whether that view had to go, but only whether the concept of responsibility could survive its excision. Now, with my developed alternative, PEC, before us, I want to end by returning to this question. Because PEC applies exclusively to acts that are wrong or foolish, one thing we must ask is whether it can be integrated into a larger account that also applies to right and prudent acts. More fundamentally, because PEC detaches an agent's responsibility from his awareness of what he is doing, there are questions about its consistency with both responsibility's voluntariness condition and the widely held view that responsibility requires control. In this final chapter, I will take up each of these challenges. Although they all raise interesting issues about responsibility, I will argue that none of them show the concept to be incoherent.

I

Let us begin with the distinction between acts that are wrong or foolish, on the one hand, and acts that are right and prudent on the other. As we have seen, it is natural to suppose that there is a single concept of responsibility that applies in both the negative and the positive contexts. However, PEC, which asserts that an unwitting wrongdoer or foolish agent satisfies responsibility's epistemic condition whenever his cognitive failure falls below some applicable standard and is caused by the interaction of his constitutive states, has no obvious analogue in the positive context. Thus, if we accept PEC, then we may seem forced to concede that our attributions of responsibility in the two contexts are not univocal after all.

To bring this difficulty into focus, it will be helpful to have an example before us. Thus, consider the following variant of *Colicky Baby*:

> *Periorbital Cellulitis.* Scout is again in charge of her sister's colicky baby, and the baby has again been crying for hours. In this variant, though, the baby also has periorbital cellulitis, a painless eye infection that can travel to the brain if not treated quickly. Although the baby's eye is grotesquely swollen, Scout does not register that anything is amiss. However, because she finds the baby's fussing intensely irritating, she takes it to a nearby Urgent Care Center to get it calmed down. There the periorbital cellulitis is noticed and treated and the baby's life is saved.

To make the parallel between the two cases as close as possible, let us suppose that Scout's evidence that the baby is seriously ill in *Periorbital Cellulitis* is just as strong as her evidence that giving it vodka will make it sick in *Colicky Baby*. Let us suppose, as well, that Scout's failure to process her evidence is equally substandard, and is equally due to her constitutive psychology, in each case. Let us suppose, finally, that in *Periorbital Cellulitis*, Scout has come to dislike the baby so much that she would *not* bring it to the Urgent Care Center if she *did* realize that its eye condition was life-threatening. Under these suppositions, the constitutive psychology that prevents Scout from recognizing the morally relevant aspect of her situation is just as much the cause of her doing the right thing in *Periorbital Cellulitis* as it is of her doing the wrong thing in *Colicky Baby*. Nevertheless, although Scout deserves blame for making the baby sick in *Colicky Baby*, she deserves no credit for saving its life in *Periorbital Cellulitis*.

Although these cases both satisfy the conditions laid down in PEC's clause (2b), the problem they pose is not restricted to PEC. The basic difficulty is that Scout seems responsible in the negative *Colicky Baby* but not in the parallel but positive *Periorbital Cellulitis*, and this difference will persist whether or not we accept PEC. However, although the difficulty is not confined to PEC, it remains pertinent to the question to which PEC is my answer—How can we best reconstruct responsibility's epistemic condition?—because it suggests that no single reconstruction can yield the right results in both sorts of case. If we accept the searchlight view, we can explain why Scout is not responsible in the positive *Periorbital Cellulitis*, but we cannot explain why she *is* responsible in the negative *Colicky Baby*; if we replace the searchlight view with PEC, we gain the ability to account for Scout's responsibility in *Colicky Baby* but lose the ability to explain why she is not responsible in *Periorbital Cellulitis*. Because no single reconstruction of the epistemic condition seems capable of capturing our intuitions about both cases, we may be led to wonder whether the same concept of responsibility applies in each.

I am not sure how deep this objection cuts. One simple answer to it is that even many concepts that do seem quite unified impose drastically different criteria for their application in different contexts. Competence at cooking has nothing to do with competence at playing point guard or writing philosophy or managing one's financial affairs, yet the same concept of competence is at work in each case. Another possible response is that many perfectly coherent concepts are *not* unified, but rather, like the concept of a game, apply to all objects that are similar enough along a great enough number of important enough dimensions. However, even if some such rejoinder is dialectically sufficient, it will not be satisfying because it will leave us without an explanation of *why* responsibility's epistemic condition takes such a different form in the positive and negative contexts. To fill this gap, I now want to offer just such an explanation—one that seeks to (re)establish the concept's unity by tracing the problematic asymmetry to a structural difference between the two contexts themselves. Because my explanation will assume that PEC is correct as far as it goes, it should, if successful, lend some further support to the case for that view.

The structural difference that I have in mind is rooted in the truism that morality and prudence are both action-guiding. Their central function is not merely to classify acts as right or wrong or prudent or imprudent, but rather to give us *reasons* to perform some acts and to avoid others. To engage with their demands, we therefore must not only do what is right and prudent, but must also do it *because* it is right and prudent. When we fall short in either way—when we either do the wrong thing or else do the right thing for the wrong reasons—we are not acting morally or prudently in the full sense. Where morality and prudence are concerned, there are two ways of getting it wrong but only one way to get it right.

And, because of this, the asymmetry between the negative and positive cases is exactly what we should expect. To see this, consider first the status of the unwitting wrongdoer. When an agent neither does the right thing nor (therefore) does it for the right reasons, his act is a definitive moral failure. Thus, as long as he himself is suitably connected to both aspects of his failure, there is no impediment to holding him responsible. In the original *Colicky Baby*, in which Scout would have done the right thing for the right reasons if her constitutive psychology had not prevented her from recognizing her act's wrong-making feature, the states that make her the person she is *are* the direct source of both aspects of her moral failure. They are the causes both of her failure to respond to her reasons for not giving vodka to the baby and, by extension, of her wrong act of giving it vodka. Moreover, even in a variant of *Colicky Baby* in which Scout would not have done the right thing for the right reasons *even if* her constitutive psychology had not prevented her from recognizing her act's wrong-making feature—a variant, for example, in which she is as annoyed at the baby as she is in *Periorbital Cellulitis*—the psychology that makes her the person she is will remain the direct source of both aspects of a moral failure to which she would have been connected in a different but equally intimate way (i.e., by consciously choosing it) in their absence. Hence, either way, there is a natural and convincing explanation of why unwitting wrongdoers such as the Scout of *Colicky Baby* seem responsible for their wrong acts.

By contrast, when someone unwittingly acts *rightly*, the situation is considerably less straightforward; for although the unwitting rightdoer has indeed satisfied one of the conditions for moral success, he has often not satisfied the other. Many unwitting rightdoers, like the Scout of *Periorbital Cellulitis*, have made no cognitive contact with the features of their acts that make them right, and so have not performed those acts for the right reasons. When the moral status of a person's act is ambiguous in this way, the import of the causal role of his constitutive psychology is ambiguous as well. On the one hand, because the agent's right act is not performed for the right reasons, the constitutive psychology that prevents him from recognizing the act's right-making feature can hardly connect him to it in a way that renders him deserving of credit or praise. On the other hand, because the agent's act is in fact right, the constitutive psychology that prevents him from recognizing its right-making feature also cannot connect him to it in a way that renders him deserving of blame or censure. Because the unwitting rightdoer's relation to his act is in this way equivocal, no definite conclusions can be drawn. Thus, the judgments that we in fact make about such agents—for example, that the Scout of *Periorbital Cellulitis* is not responsible for saving the baby—are again just what we should expect.

II

Because this unifying explanation is available, the asymmetry in our judgments about the responsibility of unwitting wrongdoers and rightdoers does not show that our concept of responsibility is too fragmented to be coherent. However, it is one thing to block this charge, and quite another to articulate a single version of the epistemic condition that applies to both sorts of agent. Thus, the natural next question is how we can transform PEC into a formula that applies in all the relevant cases.

Because PEC was introduced three chapters ago, a reminder of its wording may be helpful. What it says is

> PEC: When someone performs a wrong or foolish act in a way that satisfies the voluntariness condition, and when he also satisfies any other conditions for responsibility that are independent of the epistemic condition, he is responsible for his act's wrongness or foolishness if, but only if, he either
>
> (1) is aware that the act is wrong or foolish when he performs it, or else
>
> (2) is unaware that the act is wrong or foolish despite having evidence for its wrongness or foolishness his failure to recognize which
>   (a) falls below some applicable standard, and
>   (b) is caused by the interaction of some combination of his constitutive attitudes, dispositions, and traits.

Bearing this wording in mind, let us now ask what changes we must make to allow our formulation to apply also to right and prudent acts.

Because an agent is not responsible for his right or prudent act unless he performs that act for the right reasons, and because an agent whose failure to recognize the evidence for his act's rightness or prudence is both substandard and caused by his constitutive psychology is very often not in a position to perform the act for the right reasons, such agents often do not have enough information to satisfy responsibility's epistemic condition. For this reason, we cannot extend PEC by simply adding a reference to rightness or prudence throughout. However, because any agent who *is* aware that his act is right or prudent always *does* have all the information that he needs to satisfy responsibility's epistemic condition, we can indeed extend PEC by appending the words "or right or prudent" to the occurrence of "wrong or foolish" in its *first* clause and making the corresponding changes above. If we did this but nothing else, then we would in effect be saying that although the searchlight view does not apply in cases of wrong or foolish action, it does apply in cases of right and prudent action.

But, in fact, we must not stop here; for the class of agents who have enough information to satisfy the epistemic condition includes not only those who are fully conscious of what makes their acts right or prudent, but also some who are not. As we saw in chapter 4, even agents who are unaware of the considerations that render their acts right or prudent may sometimes perform those acts for the right reasons. Moreover, when agents act for good reasons that they do not consciously register, we standardly judge that they, too, are responsible and praiseworthy for what they do. A philosophically prominent example of an agent who seems responsible for an act whose rightness he does not recognize is Mark Twain's Huckleberry Finn, whose resistance to returning Jim to his owner is naturally viewed as an unconscious response to the demands of friendship or the evils of slavery. Some easily recognized examples from the prudential realm are the successful investor who "instinctively" purchases some stocks while avoiding others, the experienced diagnostician who recognizes his patient's condition despite the absence of clear symptoms, and the sailor who senses the onset of a storm while the sky is still a brilliant blue. In these and many similar cases, we take the agent to be responsible because we believe he acted in response to a combination of cues which he could not specify but which nevertheless gave him good reason to act as he did.[1]

When someone unconsciously registers and responds to the moral or prudential considerations that tell in favor of a certain act, he achieves a moral or prudential success. Because PEC's second clause was introduced to capture the epistemic link between an unwitting wrongdoer or foolish agent and his moral or prudential *failure*, we cannot accommodate such cases by tinkering with that clause. Instead, we must add a further clause which resembles (1) by allowing us to locate the crucial epistemic linkage in the agent's response to the reasons for acting as he did while resembling (2) by removing that linkage from the conscious realm. What we need, in other words, is a third disjunct which asserts that agents can satisfy responsibility's epistemic condition by accurately but unconsciously processing the information to which they have access.

By extending PEC's first disjunct and adding this new one, we will make the transition from a partial to a full reconstruction of responsibility's epistemic condition. When PEC is augmented in both ways, the full epistemic condition that emerges is

> FEC: When someone performs an act in a way that satisfies the voluntariness condition, and when he also satisfies any other conditions for responsibility that are independent of the epistemic condition, he is responsible for his act's morally or prudentially relevant feature if, but only if, he either
>
> (1) is consciously aware that the act has that feature (i.e., is wrong or foolish or right or prudent) when he performs it; or else
>
> (2) is unaware that the act is wrong or foolish despite having evidence for its wrongness or foolishness his failure to recognize which
>   (a) falls below some applicable standard, and
>   (b) is caused by the interaction of some combination of his constitutive attitudes, dispositions, and traits; or else
>
> (3) is unaware that the act is right or prudent despite having made enough cognitive contact with the evidence for its rightness or prudence to enable him to perform the act on that basis.

1. For rich discussion of a further array of subterranean reason-responders, see Nomy Arpaly, *Unprincipled Virtue* (Oxford: Oxford University Press, 2003), chapter 2.

Although FEC is complicated and unlovely, and although its last clause is far from precise, it offers the very significant advantages of capturing the full range of our intuitions, establishing a suitable epistemic link between an agent and each type of act for which he can be responsible, and accommodating the natural explanation of the asymmetry between our judgments about positive and negative cases. Taken together, this combination of virtues seems decisive. Thus, although there is obviously room for much further refinement, it seems safe to conclude that any adequate alternative to the searchlight view is likely to take roughly this form.

III

Despite FEC's complexity, there is nothing incoherent about its requirements. But can we say the same about the broader concept of responsibility whose epistemic condition it seeks to capture? Although some aspects of this question are obviously beyond our scope—we cannot, for example, here consider the charge that the concept is incoherent because it requires that agents create themselves *ex nihilo*—our discussion does raise questions about whether responsibility's epistemic condition can be made to mesh smoothly with its voluntariness condition.

The fit between responsibility's epistemic and voluntariness conditions is not a problem for adherents of the searchlight view, since, as I remarked in chapter 6, they can think of the searchlight of an agent's consciousness as guiding the engine of his will. However, when we replace the searchlight view with FEC, tensions between the two conditions quickly emerge. Not surprisingly, these tensions center on FEC's second and third disjuncts. They arise because an agent can satisfy FEC's second disjunct without recognizing his act's wrong- or foolish-making features and can satisfy FEC's third disjunct without recognizing his act's right or prudent-making features. These implications are significant because an agent who does not recognize his act's wrong- or imprudent-making features cannot consciously choose to perform it *despite* its wrongness or foolishness, while an agent who does not recognize his act's right- or prudent-making features cannot consciously choose to perform it *because* it is right or prudent. This means that if performing an act voluntarily involves choosing to perform it in full awareness of its morally or prudentially relevant features, then no one who satisfies FEC's second or third disjunct *can* perform his act voluntarily.

Because the whole point of introducing FEC's second and third disjuncts was to capture the intuition that agents are sometimes responsible for what they unwittingly do, the conclusion that unwitting agents cannot satisfy the voluntariness requirement, and so would not be responsible in any event, would completely undermine our rationale for adopting FEC. However, here, as above, the problem is not restricted to (what is now) FEC. The problem arises not because FEC *captures* the fact that agents often seem responsible for acts of whose morally or prudentially relevant features they are unaware, but rather, and more simply, because agents often *do* seem responsible for such acts. As long as we view agents like Alessandra, Julian, and the others as blameworthy for their unwitting misadventures, and as long as we take unconscious reason-responders like Huckleberry Finn to deserve credit for their meritorious acts, we cannot take the concept of responsibility that supports these judgments to require any form of voluntariness that in its turn requires awareness.

But can we really *avoid* taking the requisite form of voluntariness to require awareness? This suggestion is problematic because one of the main reasons for including voluntariness among the necessary conditions for responsibility is to avoid having to hold anyone responsible for what is beyond his control. The idea that no one is responsible for what is beyond his control—henceforth the control requirement—looms large in many discussions of responsibility. Thus, if responsibility's voluntariness condition is to satisfy this requirement fully, then we must interpret voluntariness as encompassing all relevant aspects of control. However, an agent who does not realize that his act has a certain feature, or that it will issue in a certain outcome, can hardly be said to exercise control with respect to that feature or outcome. Thus, insofar as our reason for accepting the voluntariness condition is to accommodate the control requirement, we may indeed seem forced to think of voluntariness as involving awareness.

In an earlier paper that anticipated the argument of this book,[2] I tried to reconcile the control requirement with our attributions

---

2. George Sher, "Out of Control," *Ethics* 116 (January 2006), 285–301.

of responsibility to Alessandra, Julian, and the others by specifying a sense in which their unwitting wrong acts *are* within their control. To exercise control in that sense, I argued, is just to be the source of one's own epistemic failure in the way that FEC's second clause requires. However, although I stand by my arguments that FEC should replace the searchlight view, I now think this linguistic recommendation was a mistake. Neil Levy brings out the difficulty nicely when he writes that

> [t]he relevant control problem arises...because we do not exercise control over anything of which we are unaware. Sher's condition explains *why* the agents in his cases are not aware of the wrongmaking features of their acts, but explaining why they are not aware of these features explains why they do not exercise relevant control: it does not restore it. Sher's solution leaves the relevant control problem untouched.[3]

As Levy correctly notes, the conception of control that I proposed in my earlier paper is simply not the one that generates the current problem.

If I am to resolve that problem, I will therefore have to take a different tack. Instead of trying to preserve the connection between responsibility and control by replacing the standard conception of control with a watered-down substitute, I will have to stick with the original conception while arguing that the control requirement itself is less fundamental than the objection assumes. Given the control requirement's wide appeal, we obviously cannot simply dismiss it. However, what we may be able to do, and what may be sufficient to disarm the objection, is to trace the appeal of the control requirement to a combination of further premises some of which can be rejected in their turn. If our commitment to the control requirement can be shown to reflect our awareness of a more abstract truth whose import we have been led to misunderstand by the allure of a false theory, then we may be able to retain what is true and important about that requirement while also retaining all of our other intuitive judgments about who is responsible for what.

---

3. Neil Levy, "Restoring Control: Comments on George Sher," *Philosophia* 36 (June 2008), 216.

IV

When we hold someone responsible for acting wrongly, the person *whom* we hold responsible is not the same as the feature of his act *for which* we hold him responsible. Because our blame and punishment are directed at an agent but are justified (if they are) by the wrong-making features of what he has done, their grounding must include some appropriate relation *between* the agent and his act's wrong-making features.[4] Analogously, because our reactions toward those whom we view as responsible for acts that are right or prudent or wrong or foolish are also directed at the agents but justified by the morally or prudentially relevant features of what they have done, the grounding of these reactions, too, must include some suitable relation between the agents and the relevant features of their acts. To capture my earlier thought that these features must somehow have their origins in the agent himself, I will refer to this as the *origination* relation.

As just stated, the requirement that we restrict an agent's responsibility to those features of his acts to which he stands in the origination relation is very abstract. However, to transform this requirement into the control requirement, we need only interpret the origination relation in a certain way. The abstract requirement becomes the control requirement as soon as we add that in order to stand in the origination relation to a given feature of a given act, an agent must choose to perform that act while fully aware that it will have that feature.

Because this way of interpreting the abstract requirement is so familiar, it may seem no less well-grounded than that requirement itself. However, it is important to realize that the interpretation is not as well grounded as what it interprets. Unlike the abstract requirement, which is forced upon us by a deep structural fact about responsibility, the proposed way of giving content to the origination relation for which the abstract requirement calls has no comparable necessity. This does not mean that the proposed interpretation cannot be defended, but it does mean that some substantive defense must in fact be forthcoming. It is, I think, precisely our ability to factor the control requirement into an incontrovertible abstract requirement and an eminently controvertible

---

4. For relevant discussion, see my *In Praise of Blame* (Oxford: Oxford University Press, 2006), chapters 2 and 3.

specification of its key notion that explains both why the control requirement is so appealing and why we can resist its appeal.

In both cases, the explanation begins to emerge as soon as we press the question of why the origination relation should be thought to require conscious choice. There are, as far as I can see, only a few live options for answering this question. One possible strategy is to appeal to the fact that each agent arrives at his decisions by deliberating from a perspective whose limits are precisely those of his consciousness. A second is to argue that it is unreasonable or unfair (or unfair because unreasonable) to hold an agent responsible for any feature of his act of which he was unaware and so could not avoid. Yet a third is to appeal to the view that responsible agents simply *are* conscious centers of rational will. But, not coincidentally, these are exactly the strategies for defending the searchlight view that were discussed at some length in chapters 3, 4, and 8.

Because the options for defending the proposed interpretation of the origination relation appear to coincide with the options for defending the searchlight view, that interpretation and that view are best regarded as different aspects of a single theory. The theory in question, moreover, is just the one against which I have been arguing throughout this book. Thus, if my arguments have been successful, they will indeed support the conclusion that the control requirement embodies a deep truth that is distorted by a false theory. Moreover—to add insult to injury—they will also allow us to account for the control requirement's allure by observing that the lines of thought that converge on the false theory are just convincing enough to be seductive. Although the relevant appeals to the deliberative perspective and its associated conceptions of fairness and the responsible self should not, on examination, convince, their superficial appeal can easily throw their conclusions into an attractive light. That they have done so is my diagnosis of the allure of both the searchlight view and the control requirement.

Because we need not accept the control requirement, we also need not accept the version of the voluntariness condition that supports it. However, it is one thing to say that we can hold onto our concept of responsibility while abandoning *this* version of the voluntariness condition, and quite another to say that we can hold onto that concept while abandoning *the voluntariness condition itself*. An agent who knew full well that certain events were occurring, but who was in no sense the author of those events, would clearly not be responsible for any aspect of them. Thus, to say that agents can be responsible for acts that they have not in *any* sense performed voluntarily would indeed be to distort our concept of responsibility beyond recognition. To complete our discussion of the concept's coherence, we must therefore ask whether any workable version of the voluntariness condition will remain available once we abandon the control requirement.

V

At first glance, the answer to this question may appear to be a clear "no"; for when an agent lacks control over what he does, his doing it cannot be an expression of his will. However, to say that someone does something voluntarily is just to say that it *is* an expression of his will. Thus, the idea of voluntarily doing what is not within one's control seems flatly contradictory.

Yet even if it is, the fact that an agent is not in control of his wrong act no more shows that that he cannot satisfy a workable version of the voluntariness condition than the fact that an agent does not know that he is acting wrongly shows that he cannot satisfy a workable version of the *knowledge* condition. In both cases, what really follows is only that if there are necessary conditions for responsibility that have to do with information and the origination of action, we cannot accurately call the first "the knowledge condition" or the second "the voluntariness condition." Just as the most plausible version of the first condition may involve epistemic considerations that sometimes do not add up to knowledge, so too may the most plausible version of the second involve considerations of origination that sometimes do not add up to voluntariness.

But is there really conceptual room for a version of (what I will continue to call) the voluntariness condition that requires neither awareness nor control? If so, what form might this version take? Because the voluntariness condition is not my central topic, I will not try to decide this question, but will merely call attention to the range of possible answers that can be found in the free will literature. As even a cursory survey makes clear, that literature contains a variety of approaches to the voluntariness condition that do not compel us to take it to require awareness, and that therefore allow us to understand it in a way that meshes with FEC. Interestingly, some of these FEC-friendly approaches are compatibilist while others are incompatibilist.

Thus, on the compatibilist side, one relevant approach begins by simply listing the factors that we standardly take to deprive agents of freedom—coercion, compulsion, insanity, and so on—and then goes on to classify any action that does not satisfy any of the cited conditions as voluntary.[5] A second takes an act to be praiseworthy or blameworthy, and hence voluntary in the relevant sense, whenever its moral quality suitably reflects the agent's character.[6] Yet a third interprets voluntariness in terms of responsiveness to reasons: it takes an agent's responsibility to depend either on whether he would act differently if presented with good reasons to do so[7] or, in one influential variant, on whether the (not necessarily conscious) mechanism that produced the action was itself reason-responsive.[8] Of these familiar compatibilist approaches, none compels us to sever the link between acting voluntarily and consciously recognizing the morally or prudentially relevant features of what one does, but each can be developed in a way that does just this. Moreover, on the incompatibilist side, the same appears to hold for Robert Kane's version of libertarianism. According to Kane, an agent's will is not free unless the antecedents of his act include uncaused microphysical events within his brain—events of whose actual nature the agent himself is of

5. In its classical form, this approach mentioned only external impediments to an agent's will; see, for example, Thomas Hobbes, *Leviathan*, ed. Edwin Curley (Indianapolis, IN: Hackett Publishing Company, 1994), part I, ch. XIV, 79. For a more recent version that extends the approach to encompass some "internal" impediments, see A. J. Ayer, "Freedom and Necessity," in Derk Pereboom, ed., *Free Will* (Indianapolis, IN: Hackett Publishing Company, 1997), 110–18.

6. The definitive statement of this view appears in David Hume, *Treatise of Human Nature*, ed. L. A. Selby-Bigge (Oxford: Oxford University Press, 1960), book II, part III, sec. II, 411. See also David Hume, *An Inquiry Concerning Human Understanding*, ed. Charles W. Hendel (Indianapolis, Ind.: Bobbs-Merrill, 1955), sec. VII, part II, 107.

7. For some variants of this approach, see Alasdair MacIntyre, "Determinism," *Mind*, 66 (1957), 28–41; Robert Nozick, *Philosophical Explanations* (Cambridge, MA: Harvard University Press, 1981); and Daniel Dennett, *Elbow Room: Varieties of Free Will Worth Wanting* (Cambridge, MA: MIT Press, 1984).

8. John Fischer and Mark Ravizza, *Responsibility and Control* (Cambridge: Cambridge University Press, 1998).

course entirely unaware.[9] Although Kane also writes that "[p]ersons experience these complex processes phenomenologically as 'efforts of will,'" this way of (re)introducing consciousness seems separable from his other and more central claim.[10] If it is, then his approach, too, will lend itself to development in a way that avoids commitment to the searchlight view. Whether any of these accounts will ultimately prove defensible is of course a further question, but given the variety of plausible alternatives, we may safely dismiss the worry that responsibility's two main conditions cannot be made to mesh.

One final version of the incoherence objection remains to be considered. It might still be argued that the connections that obtain among responsibility, voluntariness, and control are simply definitional—that it is analytically true both that agents can only exercise control over what they are aware of and that agents can only be responsible for what they can control. If both of these connections hold, then any conception of something that does not require a form of control that involves awareness will by definition not be a conception of *responsibility*. However, to this final definitional version of the objection, it seems sufficient to point out that what matters is not whether the conception at which we have arrived can be *called* "responsibility," but only whether it does all the same work, and answers to all the same needs, as one that can. As long as our conception applies only to agents who are capable of recognizing and responding to practical and theoretical reasons, as long as it applies to these agents in virtue of actions whose morally and prudentially relevant features we can retrospectively ask them to justify, and as long as it makes sense of our willingness to respond to these agents but not others by praising and giving them credit for acting prudently or doing the right thing and blaming or punishing them for acting wrongly or foolishly, the name we give it won't matter at all.

VI

The pieces of my account are now all in place. However, it is one thing to have them all before us, and quite another to see clearly how they fit

---

9. Robert Kane, *The Significance of Free Will* (New York: Oxford University Press, 1998).

10. Kane, *Significance*, 130. For a list of the sorts of conscious occurrences—Kane calls these "self-formed willings"—whose freedom is thus established, see Kane, 125.

together. To anticipate the main questions I expect readers to have, I will end by externalizing my internal critic and allowing him to quiz me. Here is my catechism.

Q: Your argument against the searchlight view rests heavily on our intuitions about the responsibility of agents like Alessandra, Julian, and the others. However, in your defense of FEC, you show no qualms about dismissing the intuition that no one is responsible for anything that is beyond his control. Of these intuitions, the latter seems at least as firm as any in the former set. Thus, in dismissing the control requirement, haven't you employed a blatant double standard?

A: The reason I don't think there's a double standard is that unlike our attributions of responsibility to Alessandra, Julian, and the others, which appear to be relatively uncontaminated by theory, our commitment to the control requirement is deeply bound up with certain theoretical commitments. As I argued above, those commitments are distinct from the abstract requirement whose content they specify, and are separated from any ground-level judgments about responsibility by a number of interpretive and explanatory layers. For this reason, we can abandon the theoretical commitments, and so too the control requirement that presupposes them, without giving up any of our ground-level judgments. It is only the latter judgments—the ones we are preanalytically inclined to make about particular cases—to which an adequate account of responsibility must (for the most part) remain true.

Q: When someone doesn't realize that he is acting wrongly or foolishly, the explanation must be either that he lacks evidence or that he has evidence but is prevented from processing it. When an agent's lack of awareness brings him below standard, he must have evidence that he fails to process, and so the explanation must be of the second kind. However, anything that prevents an agent from processing his evidence must be either a part of his psychophysical makeup or something that causally interacts with it. Thus, when the normative conjunct of FEC's disjunct (2) is satisfied, isn't the causal conjunct automatically satisfied too? And doesn't this make the causal conjunct redundant?

A: There's something right about this objection, but also something wrong. What seems right is its claim that the only sort of cognitive lapse that can fall below a standard that applies to an agent is one whose causes lie somewhere in that agent's own makeup; but what's wrong is its implication that this makes (2)'s causal conjunct redundant. As we saw in chapter 5, a reconstruction of responsibility's epistemic condition that took it to be satisfied whenever an agent should have known that he was acting wrongly or foolishly—that is, whenever (2)'s normative conjunct alone was satisfied—would leave us without an explanation of how the act's wrongness or foolishness was connected *to the agent*. The function of (2)'s causal conjunct is to supply the missing explanation. That such an explanation is available whenever (2)'s normative conjunct is satisfied is, as far as I can see, a plus rather than a minus for my account.

Q: Your account, though straightforward compared to others within analytic philosophy, is nevertheless quite complicated. It depicts responsibility as having at least two necessary conditions, it says that one of those necessary conditions can be fulfilled in three different ways, and it takes one of these ways of fulfilling that condition to have both a normative and a causal component. In specifying the causal component, it draws on a practically open-ended but theoretically well-articulated conception of the boundaries of the responsible self. No ordinary person thinks of responsibility in these terms, yet just about everyone confidently attributes it to some agents but not to others. Given this disconnect, how much contact can there be between your account and our ordinary concept of responsibility? What, exactly, is your account an account *of*?

A: Well, it's certainly not an account of what goes through our minds when we hold people responsible. You, critic, are quite right to suggest that we standardly make these judgments without running through any preparatory sequence and without working methodically through any check-list. To suppose otherwise would be to take our attributions of responsibility to involve not one, but many, thoughts too many. It is, however, quite consistent with this to say that our attributions of responsibility are *governed* by something like a check-list—that in order to have this (or any other) concept, one must be disposed to apply it only in contexts that display a (possibly logically complex) combination of features. What I take myself to be doing is giving an account of precisely the epistemic considerations that in fact structure our attributions of responsibility—one which, I hope, not only accurately identifies those considerations, but also sheds light on how they are connected and why they matter.

Q: But how much light does your account really shed on these matters? According to that account, the ways in which a person can satisfy responsibility's epistemic condition include being conscious of his act's morally or prudentially relevant features, being caused *not* to be conscious of them in a way that brings him below some appropriate standard, and nonconsciously taking them to give him reasons for acting. Consciousness, causation, and reason-responsiveness are radically different relations, and are notoriously associated with highly divergent perspectives on human beings. Given the diversity of its elements, isn't your account far too fragmented to illuminate either the unity of the concept of responsibility or its importance?

A: Just the opposite: what unifies the account's different elements is precisely that they *do* mirror the complexity of the beings to whom the concept of responsibility applies. Because those beings—that is, we ourselves—are at once inhabitants of the natural world and possessed of features that set them apart from it, we may naturally expect them to fall under concepts that reflect this complexity. Moreover, because the features that set us apart from (at least most of) the natural world include both our occupying a perspective from which we deliberate and our acting on the basis of reasons, it is only to be expected that some of these mixed concepts will apply to us in our capacity as agents. The concept of responsibility, which designates the relation between an agent and his act that makes it reasonable to praise, blame, and punish him for it, is a prime candidate for this status. By working backward from the responsible agent's conscious deliberation and judgments about reasons to the aspects of his psychology and physiology that causally sustain these activities, and by building an essential reference to these sustaining elements into FEC's second clause, I have tried to strike a balance between accepting the primary importance of the responsible agent's deliberation and judgments about reasons and acknowledging that much else about him seems relevant to our reactions to what he has done. In attempting to strike this balance, I have sought not only to accommodate the full range of intuitive judgments about who is responsible for what, but also to reconstruct the basis for those judgments in a way that does full justice to the complexity of the creatures to whom they apply.

INDEX

Anscombe, G. E. M., 4n
Aristotle, 1, 35
Arpaly, Nomy, 38n, 68n, 136n, 143n
attributionism, 120–1, 128–33
Austin, J. L., 6n
awareness, standards governing, 21, 82, 87–90, 97–115, 152
    understood as normative, 98–9, 106, 111–5
    understood as statistical, 98–99, 106–9
Ayer, A. J., 150n

benighting act, 34–7. *See also* tracing; wrongful choice, made earlier than wrongful act
Bok, Hilary, 18, 43–54
Burge, Tyler, 118n

causation *See* responsibility, role of causation in determining knowledge condition for
Chalmers, David, 118n
character, 90–1, 112–3, 122
Clark, Andy, 118n

cognitive capacities, 109–10, 113–5
consciousness, 22, 119–21, 123–8, 154
constitutive states, 20–1, 86–93, 105–6, 117–36, 140–1
    identified as sustaining rationality-related activities, 121–4
    relation to cognitive lapses, 20–1, 86–93, 105–6, 117–37
control, 19, 22, 55–60, 94, 137, 145–52

Davidson, Donald, 4n
deliberation, 10, 19, 43–54, 55, 58–9, 61, 64–5, 124, 148, 154
deliberative perspective. *See* first-person perspective
Dennett, Daniel, 150n
determinism, 1, 150–1
Donovan, D. A., 102–4
Doris, John, 108n
Dressler, Joshua, 27, 36n, 100

epistemic condition for responsibility. *See* responsibility, knowledge condition for

fairness, 11, 18–9, 55–69, 148
FEC (full epistemic condition)
    143–6, 150, 152
    formulated, 143
first-person perspective, 9–11, 41–54,
    62, 124–6. *See also* deliberation
Fischer, John Martin, 1n, 39n, 134n,
    150n
Fletcher, George P., 107n
forfeiture view, 14–5
Frankfurt, Harry, 134

Glover, Jonathan, 56n
Goldman, Alvin H., 4n

Haely, Karen, 103n
Hart, H. L. A., 26n, 80–1, 83
Herbert, A. P., 107n
Herman, Barbara, 8
Hobbes, Thomas, 150n
Holmes, Oliver Wendell,
    101n, 107n
Hubin, Donald C., 103n
Hume, David, 21n, 150n
Hurley, Susan, 15n
Hursthouse, Rosalind, 112n

identity-conferring states.
    See constitutive states
ignorance, culpable, 34

Jacobs, Jonathan, 35n

Kane, Robert, 56n, 150–1
Kant, Immanuel, 21, 42–3, 56
Kantian Principle, the, 18–9, 56–69
Kavka, Gregory, 38n
Korsgaard, Christine, 18, 43–54, 134n

Levy, Neil, 99n, 120, 129, 146

MacIntyre, Alasdair, 150n
MacKinnon, Catherine, 10n
McKenna, Michael, 39n

Mele, Alfred, 134n
Model Penal Code, 72, 80
Moody-Adams, Michele M., 99n
Moran, Mayo, 102n
Morris, Herbert, 80

Nagel, Thomas, 61–2, 65–6
Nozick, Robert, 150n

Parfit, Derek, 47
PEC (partial epistemic condition),
    formulated, 88, 141
Pound, Roscoe, 101n

Ravizza, Mark, 1n, 134n, 150n
reasonable person, 26–7, 100–4.
    See also should have known
reason-responsiveness, 22, 66–9,
    114–5, 119–24, 127–36, 154
reasons, judgments about. *See*
    attributionism
responsibility
    as practical concept, 17–8, 41–54
    for right or prudent acts, 13, 16–7,
        88, 93, 137–44
    knowledge condition for, 1–2, 7, 11,
        16, 22–3, 72, 93–4, 105, 139, 144,
        149, 154. *See also* PEC; FEC
    nonmoral, 12–6, 29–31
    role of causality within knowledge
        condition for, 20–2, 87, 121–8,
        131–3, 152–4
    voluntariness condition for, 1–2, 22,
        94, 137, 144–51
Reynolds, Osborne M., Jr., 107n
Rosen, Gideon, 33n, 99n

Sartre, Jean-Paul, 8
Scanlon, Thomas, 13–6, 68–9, 119n,
    120, 128–9
Schlossberger, Eugene, 36n
Schroeder, Timothy, 136n
searchlight control. *See* searchlight
    view, defined
searchlight view, defined, 5–6

Seavey, Warren A., 101n
self, responsible, 21, 117–36
  as conscious center of will, 124–28,
    148
should have known, 19–20, 26,
    71–84, 87, 90. *See also*
    reasonable person
Sidgwick, Henry, 8
Smith, Angela, 39n, 120, 128–31
Smith, Holly, 34
Smith, Michael, 109–10
Statman, Daniel, 56n

third-person perspective,
    9–11, 20, 45–6, 51–4, 61–2,
    124–6
Tognazzini, Neal, 39n
tracing, 39n. *See also* wrongful
    choice, made earlier than
    wrongful act; benighting act

Trianosky, Gregory, 35n

Vargas, Manuel, 39n
Volitionism, 120

Wallace, R. Jay, 57n
Watson, Gary, 35n, 129n,
    134n
Wildman, S. M., 102–4
Will, 9, 22, 94, 124–8, 149
Williams, Bernard, 56n
Williams, Glanville, 101n
Wolf, Susan, 136n
wrongful choice, made earlier
    than wrongful act, 25, 34–9,
    82–3. *See also* benighting act;
    tracing

Zimmerman, Michael J., 8, 33n, 34n